OXFORD STUDENT TEXTS

Series Editor: Victor Lee

THE RAPE OF THE LOCK

Alexander Pope

The Rape
of the Lock

Edited by Elizabeth Gurr

Oxford University Press

OXFORD
UNIVERSITY PRESS

Great Clarendon Street, Oxford OX2 6DP

Oxford University Press is a department of the University of Oxford.
It furthers the University's objective of excellence in research, scholarship,
and education by publishing worldwide in

Oxford New York

Auckland Bangkok Buenos Aires Cape Town Chennai
Dar es Salaam Delhi Hong Kong Istanbul Karachi Kolkata
Kuala Lumpur Madrid Melbourne Mexico City Mumbai
Nairobi São Paulo Shanghai Taipei Tokyo Toronto

Oxford is a registered trade mark of Oxford University Press
in the UK and in certain other countries

First published 1990
10 9 8 7 6

ISBN 0 19 831958 4

Typeset by Pentancor PLC. High Wycombe, Bucks.
Printed in China

Other titles in the series:

Contents

Acknowledgements

The text of this edition was first published by OUP in 1966, edited by J. S. Cunningham. I have followed his edition, I hope faithfully, and I record here my thanks. His edition derived principally from the great Twickenham edition by Geoffrey Tillotson to whose meticulous scholarship all subsequent Pope editors are deeply indebted.

It will be apparent from the Notes and Approaches that the work of many critics has influenced the preparation of this edition. Therefore, I would like this acknowledgement to serve as a general tribute to all those who have acted as sources of inspiration.

Finally, I would like to thank Dr Victor Lee, the general editor of the series, for his wit and encouragement which guided this book throughout.

Elizabeth Gurr

Editors

Dr Victor Lee

Dr Victor Lee, the Series Editor, read English at University College, Cardiff. He was awarded a doctorate at Oxford University. He has experience of teaching at Secondary and Tertiary level, and is currently working at the Open University. Victor Lee has been Chief Examiner in English for three examination boards over a period of twenty years.

Elizabeth Gurr

Elizabeth Gurr was born in New Zealand and educated there and at Oxford. She has taught in schools, colleges and universities in England and Africa and is currently Head of English at a comprehensive school in Berkshire. She is married with three sons and the author of *Alexander Pope* in the Writer and Critics series (Oliver and Boyd).

The publishers would like to thank the following for
permission to reproduce illustrations:

The British Library p. 117 (bottom), 118, 119, 120; the
Trustees of the British Museum p. 116; the Courtauld
Institute of Art, Witt Library p. 115; the Victoria and
Albert Museum Picture Library p. 117 (top).

The cover illustration is by John Rushton

Foreword

Oxford Student Texts are specifically aimed at presenting poetry and drama to an audience which is studying English Literature at an advanced level. Each text is designed as an integrated whole consisting of three parts. The poetry or the play is always placed first to stress its importance and to encourage students to enjoy it without secondary critical material of any kind. When help is needed on other occasions, the second and third parts of these texts, the Notes and the Approaches provide it.

The Notes perform two functions. Firstly, they provide information and explain allusions. Secondly, and this is where they differ from most texts at this level, they often raise questions of central concern to the interpretation of the poem or the play being dealt with, particularly in the use of a general note placed at the beginning of the particular note.

The third part, the Approaches section, deals with major issues of response to the particular selection of poetry or drama, as opposed to the work of the writer as a whole. One of the major aims of this part of the text is to emphasize that there is no one right answer to interpretations, but a series of approaches. Readers are given guidance as to what counts as evidence, but, in the end, left to make up their mind as to which are the most suitable interpretations, or to add their own.

To help achieve this, the Approaches section contains a number of activity-discussion sequences, although it must be stressed that these are optional. Significant issues about the poetry or the play are raised in these activities. The reader is invited to tackle these activities before proceeding to the discussion section where possible responses to the questions raised in the activities are considered. Their main function is to engage the reader actively in the ideas of the text. However, these activity-discussion sequences are so arranged that, if readers wish to treat the Approaches as continuous prose and not attempt the activities, they can.

At the end of each text there is also a list of tasks. Whereas the activity-discussion sequences are aimed at increasing understanding of the literary work itself, these tasks are intended to help explore ideas about the poetry or the play after the student has completed the reading of the poems and the studying of the Notes and Approaches. These tasks are particularly helpful for course-work projects or in preparing for an examination.

Victor Lee   *Series Editor*

The Rape of the Lock

The Rape of the Lock
an Heroi-comical Poem

Nolueram, Belinda, tuos violare capillos;
Sed juvat hoc precibus me tribuisse tuis.
MART.

To
Mrs. Arabella Fermor

Madam,

It will be in vain to deny that I have some regard for this piece, since I dedicate it to You. Yet you may bear me witness, it was intended only to divert a few young Ladies, who have good sense and good humour enough to laugh not only at their sex's little unguarded follies, but at their own. But as it was communicated with the air of a Secret, it soon found its way into the world. An imperfect copy having been offer'd to a Bookseller, you had the good-nature for my sake to consent to the publication of one more correct: This I was forc'd to, before I had executed half my design, for the Machinery was entirely wanting to compleat it.

The Machinery, Madam, is a term invented by the Critics, to signify that part which the Deities, Angels, or Dæmons are made to act in a Poem: for the ancient Poets are in one respect like many modern Ladies; let an action be never so trivial in itself, they always make it appear of the utmost importance. These Machines I determin'd to raise on a very new and odd foundation, the *Rosicrucian* doctrine of Spirits.

I know how disagreeable it is to make use of hard words before a Lady; but 'tis so much the concern of a Poet to have his works understood, and particularly by your Sex, that you must give me leave to explain two or three difficult terms.

The *Rosicrucians* are a people I must bring you acquainted with. The best account I know of them is in a French book call'd *Le Comte de Gabalis*, which both in its title and size is so like a Novel, that many of the Fair Sex have read it for one by mistake.

According to these Gentlemen, the four Elements are inhabited by Spirits, which they call *Sylphs, Gnomes, Nymphs,* and *Salamanders.* The *Gnomes* or Dæmons of Earth delight in mischief; but the *Sylphs,* whose habitation is in the Air, are the best-condition'd creatures imaginable. For they say, any mortals may enjoy the most intimate familiarities with these gentle Spirits, upon a condition very easy to all true Adepts, an inviolate preservation of Chastity.

As to the following Canto's, all the passages of them are as fabulous, as the Vision at the beginning, or the Transformation at the end; (except the loss of your Hair, which I always mention with reverence.) The Human persons are as fictitious as the Airy ones; and the character of *Belinda,* as it is now manag'd, resembles you in nothing but in Beauty.

If this Poem had as many Graces as there are in your Person, or in your Mind, yet I could never hope it should pass thro' the world half so Uncensur'd as You have done. But let its fortune be what it will, mine is happy enough, to have given me this occasion of assuring you that I am, with the truest esteem,

MADAM,

Your most obedient,
Humble Servant
A. POPE.

The Rape of the Lock

Canto I

What dire offence from am'rous causes springs,
What mighty contests rise from trivial things,
I sing—This verse to *Caryll*, Muse! is due:
This, ev'n *Belinda* may vouchsafe to view:
Slight is the subject, but not so the praise,
If She inspire, and He approve my lays.
  Say what strange motive, Goddess! could compel
A well-bred Lord t'assault a gentle *Belle*?
Oh say what stranger cause, yet unexplor'd,
10 Cou'd make a gentle *Belle* reject a Lord?
In tasks so bold, can little men engage,
And in soft bosoms dwells such mighty Rage?
  Sol thro' white curtains shot a tim'rous ray,
And ope'd those eyes that must eclipse the day;
Now lap-dogs give themselves the rousing shake,
And sleepless lovers, just at twelve, awake:
Thrice rung the bell, the slipper knock'd the ground,
And the press'd watch return'd a silver sound.
Belinda still her downy pillow prest,
20 Her guardian *Sylph* prolong'd the balmy rest:
'Twas he had summon'd to her silent bed
The morning-dream that hover'd o'er her head.
A Youth more glitt'ring than a Birth-night Beau,
(That ev'n in slumber caus'd her cheek to glow)
Seem'd to her ear his winning lips to lay,
And thus in whispers said, or seem'd to say.
  Fairest of mortals, thou distinguish'd care
Of thousand bright Inhabitants of Air!
If e'er one Vision touch'd thy infant thought,
30 Of all the Nurse and all the Priest have taught;

Of airy Elves by moonlight shadows seen,
The silver token, and the circled green,
Or virgins visited by Angel-pow'rs,
With golden crowns and wreaths of heav'nly flow'rs;
Hear and believe! thy own importance know,
Nor bound thy narrow views to things below.
Some secret truths, from learned pride conceal'd,
To Maids alone and Children are reveal'd:
What tho' no credit doubting Wits may give?
40 The Fair and Innocent shall still believe.
Know then, unnumber'd Spirits round thee fly,
The light Militia of the lower sky;
These, tho' unseen, are ever on the wing,
Hang o'er the Box, and hover round the Ring:
Think what an Equipage thou hast in Air,
And view with scorn two Pages and a Chair.
As now your own, our beings were of old,
And once inclos'd in Woman's beauteous mold;
Thence, by a soft transition, we repair
50 From earthly Vehicles to these of air.
Think not, when Woman's transient breath is fled,
That all her vanities at once are dead:
Succeeding vanities she still regards,
And tho' she plays no more, o'erlooks the cards.
Her joy in gilded Chariots, when alive,
And love of *Ombre,* after death survive.
For when the Fair in all the pride expire,
To their first Elements the Souls retire:
The Sprites of fiery Termagants in Flame
60 Mount up, and take a *Salamander's* name.
Soft yielding minds to Water glide away,
And sip, with *Nymphs,* their elemental Tea.
The graver Prude sinks downward to a *Gnome,*
In search of mischief still on Earth to roam.
The light Coquettes in *Sylphs* aloft repair,

And sport and flutter in the fields of Air.
   Know farther yet; whoever fair and chaste
Rejects mankind, is by some *Sylph* embrac'd:
For Spirits, freed from mortal laws, with ease
70 Assume what sexes and what shapes they please.
What guards the purity of melting Maids
In courtly balls, and midnight masquerades,
Safe from the treach'rous friend, the daring spark,
The glance by day, the whisper in the dark,
When kind occasion prompts their warm desires,
When music softens, and when dancing fires?
'Tis but their *Sylph*, the wise Celestials know,
Tho' *Honour* is the word with Men below.
   Some nymphs there are, too conscious of their face,
80 For life predestin'd to the *Gnomes* embrace.
These swell their prospects and exalt their pride,
When offers are disdain'd, and love deny'd:
Then gay Ideas crowd the vacant brain,
While Peers and Dukes, and all their sweeping train,
And Garters, Stars, and Coronets appear,
And in soft sounds, *Your Grace* salutes their ear.
'Tis these that early taint the female soul,
Instruct the eyes of young Coquettes to roll,
Teach Infant-cheeks a bidden blush to know,
90 And little hearts to flutter at a Beau.
   Oft when the world imagine women stray,
The Sylphs thro' mystic mazes guide their way,
Thro' all the giddy circle they pursue,
And old impertinence expel by new.
What tender maid but must a victim fall
To one man's treat, but for another's ball?
When *Florio* speaks, what virgin could withstand,
If gentle *Damon* did not squeeze her hand?
With varying vanities, from ev'ry part,
100 They shift the moving Toyshop of their heart;

Where wigs with wigs, with sword-knots sword-knots strive,
Beaus banish beaus, and coaches coaches drive.
This erring mortals Levity may call,
Oh blind to truth! the *Sylphs* contrive it all.

    Of these am I, who thy protection claim,
A watchful sprite, and *Ariel* is my name.
Late, as I rang'd the crystal wilds of air,
In the clear Mirror of thy ruling Star
I saw, alas! some dread event impend,

110 Ere to the main this morning sun descend.
But heav'n reveals not what, or how, or where:
Warn'd by the *Sylph*, oh pious maid, beware!
This to disclose is all thy guardian can.
Beware of all, but most beware of Man!

    He said; when *Shock*, who thought she slept too long,
Leap'd up, and wak'd his mistress with his tongue.
'Twas then *Belinda*, if report say true,
Thy eyes first open'd on a Billet-doux;

120 Wounds, Charms, and Ardors, were no sooner read,
But all the Vision vanish'd from thy head.

    And now, unveil'd, the Toilet stands display'd,
Each silver Vase in mystic order laid.
First, rob'd in white, the nymph intent adores,
With head uncover'd, the Cosmetic pow'rs.
A heav'nly Image in the glass appears,
To that she bends, to that her eyes she rears;
Th'inferior Priestess, at her altar's side,
Trembling, begins the sacred rites of Pride.
Unnumber'd treasures ope at once, and here

130 The various off'rings of the world appear;
From each she nicely culls with curious toil,
And decks the Goddess with the glitt'ring spoil.
This casket *India's* glowing gems unlocks,
And all *Arabia* breathes from yonder box.
The Tortoise here and Elephant unite,

Tranform'd to combs, the speckled, and the white.
Here files of pins extend their shining rows,
Puffs, Powders, Patches, Bibles, Billet-doux.
Now awful Beauty puts on all its arms;
140 The fair each moment rises in her charms,
Repairs her smiles, awakens ev'ry grace,
And calls forth all the wonders of her face;
Sees by degrees a purer blush arise,
And keener lightnings quicken in her eyes.
The busy *Sylphs* surround their darling care,
These set the head, and those divide the hair,
Some fold the sleeve, while others plait the gown;
And *Betty's* prais'd for labours not her own.

Canto II

Not with more glories, in th'etherial plain,
The Sun first rises o'er the purpled main,
Than issuing forth, the rival of his beams
Lanch'd on the bosom of the silver *Thames*.
Fair Nymphs, and well-drest Youths around her shone,
But ev'ry eye was fix'd on her alone.
On her white breast a sparkling Cross she wore,
Which Jews might kiss, and Infidels adore.
Her lively looks a sprightly mind disclose,
10 Quick as her eyes, and as unfix'd as those:
Favours to none, to all she smiles extends,
Oft she rejects, but never once offends.
Bright as the sun, her eyes the gazers strike,
And, like the sun, they shine on all alike.
Yet graceful ease, and sweetness void of pride
Might hide her faults, if *Belles* had faults to hide:

7

If to her share some female errors fall,
Look on her face, and you'll forget 'em all.
    This Nymph, to the destruction of mankind,
20 Nourish'd two Locks, which graceful hung behind
In equal curls, and well conspir'd to deck
With shining ringlets the smooth iv'ry neck:
Love in these labyrinths his slaves detains,
And mighty hearts are held in slender chains.
With hairy sprindges we the birds betray,
Slight lines of hair surprize the finny prey,
Fair tresses man's imperial race insnare,
And beauty draws us with a single hair.
    Th' advent'rous Baron the bright locks admir'd,
30 He saw, he wish'd, and to the prize aspir'd.
Resolv'd to win, he meditates the way,
By force to ravish, or by fraud betray;
For when success a Lover's toil attends,
Few ask, if fraud or force attain'd his ends.
    For this, ere *Phœbus* rose, he had implor'd
Propitious heav'n, and ev'ry pow'r ador'd,
But chiefly Love—to Love an altar built,
Of twelve vast *French* Romances, neatly gilt.
There lay three garters, half a pair of gloves;
40 And all the trophies of his former loves.
With tender Billet-doux he lights the pyre,
And breathes three am'rous sighs to raise the fire.
Then prostrate falls, and begs with ardent eyes
Soon to obtain, and long possess the prize:
The Pow'rs gave ear, and granted half his pray'r,
The rest, the winds dispers'd in empty air.
    But now secure the painted vessel glides,
The sun-beams trembling on the floating tydes;
While melting music steals upon the sky,
50 And soften'd sounds along the waters die;
Smooth flow the waves, the Zephyrs gently play,

Belinda smil'd, and all the world was gay.
All but the *Sylph*—with careful thoughts opprest,
Th'impending woe sate heavy on his breast.
He summons strait his Denizens of air;
The lucid squadrons round the sails repair:
Soft o'er the shrouds aërial whispers breathe,
That seem'd but Zephyrs to the train beneath.
Some to the sun their insect-wings unfold,
60 Waft on the breeze, or sink in clouds of gold;
Transparent forms, too fine for mortal sight,
Their fluid bodies half dissolv'd in light.
Loose to the wind their airy garments flew,
Thin glitt'ring textures of the filmy dew,
Dipt in the richest tincture of the skies,
Where light disports in ever-mingling dyes,
While ev'ry beam new transient colours flings,
Colours that change whene'er they wave their wings.
Amid the circle, on the gilded mast,
70 Superior by the head, was *Ariel* plac'd;
His purple pinions opening to the sun,
He rais'd his azure wand, and thus begun.
    Ye *Sylphs* and *Sylphids,* to your chief give ear,
Fays, Fairies, Genii, Elves, and *Dæmons* hear!
Ye know the spheres and various tasks assign'd
By laws eternal to th'aërial kind.
Some in the fields of purest *Æther* play,
And bask and whiten in the blaze of day.
Some guide the course of wand'ring orbs on high,
80 Or roll the planets thro' the boundless sky.
Some less refin'd, beneath the moon's pale light
Pursue the stars that shoot athwart the night,
Or suck the mists in grosser air below,
Or dip their pinions in the painted bow,
Or brew fierce tempests on the wintry main,
Or o'er the glebe distil the kindly rain.

9

Others on earth o'er human race preside,
Watch all their ways, and all their actions guide:
Of these the chief the care of Nations own,
90 And guard with Arms divide the *British* Throne.
　　Our humbler province is to tend the Fair;
Not a less pleasing, tho' less glorious care:
To save the powder from too rude a gale,
Nor let th'imprison'd essences exhale;
To draw fresh colours from the vernal flow'rs;
To steal from rainbows ere they drop in show'rs
A brighter wash; to curl their waving hairs,
Assist their blushes, and inspire their airs;
Nay oft, in dreams, invention we bestow,
100 To change a Flounce, or add a Furbelow.
　　This day, black Omens threat the brightest Fair
That e'er deserv'd a watchful spirit's care;
Some dire disaster, or by force or slight;
But what, or where, the fates have wrapt in night.
Whether the nymph shall break *Diana's* law,
Or some frail *China* jar receive a flaw,
Or stain her honour, or her new brocade,
Forget her pray'rs, or miss a masquerade,
Or lose her heart, or necklace, at a ball;
110 Or whether Heav'n has doom'd that *Shock* must fall.
Haste then, ye spirits! to your charge repair;
The flutt'ring fan be *Zephyretta's* care;
The drops to thee, *Brillante*, we consign;
And, *Momentilla*, let the watch be thine;
Do thou, *Crispissa*, tend her fav'rite Lock;
Ariel himself shall be the guard of *Shock*.
　　To fifty chosen *Sylphs*, of special note,
We trust th' important charge, the Petticoat:
Oft have we known that seven-fold fence to fail,
120 Tho' stiff with hoops, and arm'd with ribs of whale.
Form a strong line about the silver bound,

10

And guard the wide circumference around.
　　Whatever spirit, careless of his charge,
His post neglects, or leaves the fair at large,
Shall feel sharp vengeance soon o'ertake his sins,
Be stop'd in vials, or transfix'd with pins;
Or plung'd in lakes of bitter washes lie,
Or wedg'd whole ages in a bodkin's eye:
Gums and Pomatums shall his flight restrain,
130　While clog'd he beats his silken wings in vain;
Or Alom stypticks with contracting pow'r
Shrink his thin essence like a rivell'd flow'r:
Or as *Ixion* fix'd, the wretch shall feel
The giddy motion of the whirling Mill,
In fumes of burning Chocolate shall glow,
And tremble at the sea that froaths below!
　　He spoke; the spirits from the sails descend;
Some, orb in orb, around the nymph extend;
Some thrid the mazy ringlets of her hair;
140　Some hang upon the pendants of her ear;
With beating hearts the dire event they wait,
Anxious, and trembling for the birth of Fate.

Canto III

Close by those meads, for ever crown'd with flow'rs,
Where *Thames* with pride surveys his rising tow'rs,
There stands a structure of majestic frame,
Which from the neighb'ring *Hampton* takes it name.
Here *Britain's* statesmen oft the fall foredoom
Of foreign Tyrants, and of Nymphs at home;
Here thou, great ANNA! whom three realms obey,
Dost sometimes counsel take—and sometimes Tea.
　　Hither the heroes and the nymphs resort,
10　To taste a while the pleasures of a Court;

In various talk th'instructive hours they past,
Who gave the ball, or paid the visit last;
One speaks the glory of the *British* Queen,
And one describes a charming *Indian* screen;
A third interprets motions, looks, and eyes;
At ev'ry word a reputation dies.
Snuff, or the fan, supply each pause of chat,
With singing, laughing, ogling, and all that.
   Mean while declining from the noon of day,
20 The sun obliquely shoots his burning ray;
The hungry Judges soon the sentence sign,
And wretches hang that jury-men may dine;
The merchant from th'*Exchange* returns in peace,
And the long labours of the Toilet cease.
Belinda now, whom thirst of fame invites,
Burns to encounter two advent'rous Knights,
At *Ombre* singly to decide their doom;
And swells her breast with conquests yet to come.
Strait the three bands prepare in arms to join,
30 Each band the number of the sacred nine.
Soon as she spreads her hand, th'aërial guard
Descend, and sit on each important card:
First *Ariel* perch'd upon a Matadore,
Then each, according to the rank they bore;
For *Sylphs*, yet mindful of their ancient race,
Are, as when women, wondrous fond of place.
   Behold, four Kings in majesty rever'd,
With hoary whiskers and a forky beard;
And four fair Queens whose hands sustain a flow'r,
40 Th'expressive emblem of their softer pow'r;
Four Knaves in garbs succinct, a trusty band,
Caps on their heads, and halberts in their hand;
And particolour'd troops, a shining train,
Draw forth to combat on the velvet plain.
   The skilful Nymph reviews her force with care:

Let Spades be trumps! she said, and trumps they were.
   Now move to war her sable Matadores,
In show like leaders of the swarthy Moors.
Spadillio first, unconquerable Lord!
50   Led off two captive trumps, and swept the board.
As many more *Manillio* forc'd to yield,
And march'd a victor from the verdant field.
Him *Basto* follow'd, but his fate more hard
Gain'd but one trump and one *Plebeian* card.
With his broad sabre next, a chief in years,
The hoary Majesty of Spades appears,
Puts forth one manly leg, to sight reveal'd,
The rest, his many-coloured robe conceal'd.
The rebel Knave, who dares his prince engage,
60   Proves the just victim of his royal rage.
Ev'n mighty *Pam*, that Kings and Queens o'erthrew
And mow'd down armies in the fights of *Lu*,
Sad chance of war! now destitute of aid,
Falls undistinguish'd by the victor Spade!
   Thus far both armies to *Belinda* yield;
Now to the Baron fate inclines the field.
His warlike *Amazon* her host invades,
Th'imperial consort of the crown of Spades.
The Club's black Tyrant first her victim dy'd,
70   Spite of his haughty mien, and barb'rous pride:
What boots the regal circle on his head,
His giant limbs, in state unwieldy spread;
That long behind he trails his pompous robe,
And, of all monarchs, only grasps the globe?
   The Baron now his Diamonds pours apace;
Th'embroider'd King who shows but half his face,
And his refulgent Queen, with powr's combin'd,
Of broken troops an easy conquest find.
Clubs, Diamonds, Hearts, in wild disorder seen,
80   With throngs promiscuous strow the level green.

13

Thus when dispers'd a routed army runs,
Of *Asia's* troops, and *Afric's* sable sons,
With like confusion different nations fly,
Of various habit, and of various dye,
The pierc'd batallions dis-united fall,
In heaps on heaps; one fate o'erwhelms them all.
   The Knave of Diamonds tries his wily arts,
And wins (oh shameful chance!) the Queen of Hearts.
At this, the blood the virgin's cheek forsook,
90 A livid paleness spreads o'er all her look;
She sees, and trembles at th' approaching ill,
Just in the jaws of ruin, and *Codille*.   *winning trick*
And now, (as oft in some distemper'd State)
On one nice Trick depends the gen'ral fate.
An Ace of Hearts steps forth: The King unseen
Lurk'd in her hand, and mourn'd his captive Queen:
He springs to vengeance with an eager pace,
And falls like thunder on the prostrate Ace.
The nymph exulting fills with shouts the sky;
100 The walls, the woods, and long canals reply.
   Oh thoughtless mortals! ever blind to fate,
Too soon dejected, and too soon elate!
Sudden, these honours shall be snatch'd away,
And curs'd for ever this victorious day.
   For lo! the board with cups and spoons is crown'd,
The berries crackle, and the mill turns round;
On shining Altars of *Japan* they raise
The silver lamp; the fiery spirits blaze:
From silver spouts the grateful liquors glide,
110 While *China's* earth receives the smoaking tyde:
At once they gratify their scent and taste,
And frequent cups prolong the rich repaste.
Strait hover round the Fair her airy band;
Some, as she sipp'd, the fuming liquor fann'd,
Some o'er her lap their careful plumes display'd,

Trembling, and conscious of the rich brocade.
Coffee, (which makes the politician wise,
And see thro' all things with his half-shut eyes)
Sent up in vapours to the Baron's brain
120   New stratagems, the radiant Lock to gain.
Ah cease, rash youth! desist ere 'tis too late,
Fear the just Gods, and think of Scylla's Fate!
Chang'd to a bird, and sent to flit in air,
She dearly pays for *Nisus'* injur'd hair!
    But when to mischief mortals bend their will,
How soon they find fit instruments of ill?
Just then, *Clarissa* drew with tempting grace
A two-edg'd weapon from her shining case;
So Ladies in Romance assist their Knight,
130   Present the spear, and arm him for the fight.
He takes the gift with rev'rence, and extends
The little engine on his finger's ends;
This just behind *Belinda's* neck he spread,
As o'er the fragrant steams she bends her head.
Swift to the Lock a thousand Sprites repair,
A thousand wings, by turns, blow back the hair;
And thrice they twitch'd the diamond in her ear;
Thrice she look'd back, and thrice the foe drew near.
Just in that instance, anxious *Ariel* sought
140   The close recesses of the Virgin's thought;
As on the nosegay in her breast reclin'd,
He watch'd th' Ideas rising in her mind,
Sudden he view'd, in spite of all her art,
An earthly Lover lurking at her heart.
Amaz'd, confus'd, he found his pow'r expir'd,
Resign'd to fate, and with a sigh retir'd.
    The Peer now spreads the glitt'ring *Forfex* wide,
T'inclose the Lock; now joins it, to divide.
Ev'n then, before the fatal engine clos'd,
150   A wretched *Sylph* too fondly interpos'd;

15

Fate urg'd the sheers, and cut the *Sylph* in twain,
(But airy substance soon unites again)
The meeting points the sacred hair dissever
From the fair head, for ever, and for ever!
   Then flash'd the living lightning from her eyes,
And screams of horror rend th'affrighted skies.
Not louder shrieks to pitying heav'n are cast,
When husbands or when lapdogs breathe their last;
Or when rich *China* vessels fall'n from high,
160 In glitt'ring dust, and painted fragments lie!
   Let wreaths of triumph now my temples twine,
(The Victor cry'd) the glorious Prize is mine!
While fish in streams, or birds delight in air,
Or in a Coach and six the *British* Fair,
As long as *Atalantis* shall be read,
Or the small pillow grace a Lady's bed,
While visits shall be paid on solemn days,
When num'rous wax-lights in bright order blaze,
While nymphs take treats, or assignations give,
170 So long my honour, name, and praise shall live!
   What Time wou'd spare, from Steel receives its date,
And monuments, like men, submit to fate!
Steel could the labour of the Gods destroy,
And strike to dust th'imperial tow'rs of *Troy*;
Steel could the works of mortal pride confound,
And hew triumphal arches to the ground.
What wonder then, fair nymph! thy hairs shou'd feel
The conqu'ring force of unresisted steel?

Canto IV

But anxious cares the pensive nymph oppress'd,
And secret passions labour'd in her breast.
Not youthful kings in battle seiz'd alive,

Not scornful virgins who their charms survive,
Not ardent lovers robb'd of all their bliss,
Not ancient ladies when refus'd a kiss,
Not tyrants fierce that unrepenting die,
Not *Cynthia* when her manteau's pinn'd awry,
E'er felt such rage, resentment, and despair,
10 As thou, sad Virgin! for thy ravish'd Hair.
    For, that sad moment, when the *Sylphs* withdrew,
And *Ariel* weeping from *Belinda* flew,
Umbriel, a dusky, melancholy sprite,
As ever sully'd the fair face of light,
Down to the central earth, his proper scene,
Repair'd to search the gloomy Cave of *Spleen*.
    Swift on his sooty pinions flits the *Gnome*,
And in a vapour reach'd the dismal dome.
No chearful breeze this sullen region knows,
20 The dreaded East is all the wind that blows.
Here in a grotto, shelter'd close from air,
And screen'd in shades from day's detested glare,
She sighs for ever on her pensive bed,
Pain at her side, and *Megrim* at her head.
    Two handmaids wait the throne: alike in place,
But diff'ring far in figure and in face.
Here stood *Ill-nature* like an ancient maid,
Her wrinkled form in black and white array'd;
With store of pray'rs, for mornings, nights, and noons,
30 Her hand is fill'd; her bosom with lampoons.
    There *Affectation*, with a sickly mien,
Shows in her cheek the roses of eighteen,
Practis'd to lisp, and hang the head aside,
Faints into airs, and languishes with pride,
On the rich quilt sinks with becoming woe,
Wrapt in a gown, for sickness and for show.
The fair-ones feel such maladies as these,
When each new night-dress gives a new disease.

17

A constant Vapour o'er the palace flies;
40   Strange phantoms rising as the mists arise;
Dreadful, as hermit's dreams in haunted shades,
Or bright, as visions of expiring maids.
Now glaring fiends, and snakes on rolling spires,
Pale spectres, gaping tombs, and purple fires:
Now lakes of liquid gold, *Elysian* scenes,
And crystal domes, and Angels in machines.
Unnumber'd throngs on ev'ry side are seen,
Of bodies chang'd to various forms by Spleen.
Here living Tea-pots stand, one arm held out,
50   One bent; the handle this, and that the spout:
A Pipkin there, like *Homer's* Tripod walks;
Here sighs a Jar, and there a Goose-pye talks;
Men prove with child, as pow'rful fancy works,
And maids turn'd bottles, call aloud for corks.
Safe past the *Gnome* thro' this fantastic band,
A branch of healing Spleenwort in his hand.
Then thus address'd the pow'r—Hail wayward Queen!
Who rule the sex to fifty from fifteen:
Parent of vapours and of female wit,
60   Who give th' hysteric, or poetic fit,
On various tempers act by various ways,
Make some take physic, others scribble plays;
Who cause the proud their visits to delay,
And send the godly in a pett, to pray.
A Nymph there is, that all thy pow'r disdains,
And thousands more in equal mirth maintains.
But oh! if e'er thy *Gnome* could spoil a grace,
Or raise a pimple on a beauteous face,
Like Citron-waters matrons cheeks inflame,
70   Or change complexions at a losing game;
If e'er with airy horns I planted heads,
Or rumpled petticoats, or tumbled beds,
Or caus'd suspicion when no soul was rude,

Or discompos'd the head-dress of a Prude,
Or e'er to costive lap-dog gave disease,
Which not the tears of brightest eyes could ease:
Hear me, and touch *Belinda* with chagrin:
That single act gives half the world the spleen.
   The Goddess with a discontented air
80 Seems to reject him, tho' she grants his pray'r.
A wond'rous Bag with both her hands she binds,
Like that where once *Ulysses* held the winds;
There she collects the force of female lungs,
Sighs, sobs, and passions, and the war of tongues.
A Vial next she fills with fainting fears,
Soft sorrows, melting griefs, and flowing tears.
The *Gnome* rejoicing bears her gifts away,
Spreads his black wings, and slowly mounts to day.
   Sunk in *Thalestris'* arms the nymph he found,
90 Her eyes dejected and her hair unbound.
Full o'er their heads the swelling bag he rent,
And all the Furies issued at the vent.
Belinda burns with more than mortal ire,
And fierce *Thalestris* fans the rising fire.
O wretched maid! she spread her hands, and cry'd,
(While *Hampton's* echoes, wretched maid! reply'd)
Was it for this you took such constant care
The bodkin, comb, and essence to prepare?
For this your locks in paper durance bound,
100 For this with tort'ring irons wreath'd around?
For this with fillets strain'd your tender head,
And bravely bore the double loads of lead?
Gods! shall the ravisher display your hair,
While the Fops envy, and the Ladies stare!
Honour forbid! at whose unrival'd shrine
Ease, pleasure, virtue, all, our sex resign.
Methinks already I your tears survey,
Already hear the horrid things they say,

Already see you a degraded toast,
110 And all your honour in a whisper lost!
How shall I, then, your helpless fame defend?
'Twill then be infamy to seem your friend!
And shall this prize, th' inestimable prize,
Expos'd thro' crystal to the gazing eyes,
And heightened by the diamond's circling rays,
On that rapacious hand for ever blaze?
Sooner shall grass in *Hyde-Park Circus* grow,
And wits take lodgings in the sound of *Bow*;
Sooner let earth, air, sea, to *Chaos* fall,
120 Men, monkeys, lap-dogs, parrots, perish all!
    She said; then raging to Sir *Plume* repairs,
And bids her Beau demand the precious hairs:
(Sir *Plume*, of amber Snuff-box justly vain,
And the nice conduct of a clouded cane)
With earnest eyes, and round unthinking face,
He first the snuff-box open'd, then the case,
And thus broke out—"My Lord, why, what the devil?
"Z——ds! damn the lock! 'fore Gad, you must be civil!
"Plague on't! 'tis past a jest—nay prithee, pox!
130 "Give her the hair"—he spoke, and rapp'd his box.
    It grieves me much (reply'd the Peer again)
Who speaks so well should ever speak in vain.
But by this Lock, this sacred Lock I swear,
(Which never more shall join its parted hair;
Which never more its honours shall renew,
Clip'd from the lovely head where late it grew)
That while my nostrils draw the vital air,
This hand which won it, shall for ever wear.
He spoke, and speaking, in proud triumph spread
140 The long-contended honours of her head.
    But *Umbriel*, hateful *Gnome*! forbears not so;
He breaks the Vial whence the sorrows flow.
Then see! the nymph in beauteous grief appears,

Her eyes half-languishing, half-drown'd in tears;
On her heav'd bosom hung her drooping head,
Which, with a sigh, she rais'd; and thus she said.
    For ever curs'd be this detested day,
Which snatch'd my best, my fav'rite curl away!
Happy! ah ten times happy had I been,
150   If *Hampton-Court* these eyes had never seen!
Yet am not I the first mistaken maid,
By love of Courts to num'rous ills betray'd.
Oh had I rather un-admir'd remain'd
In some lone isle, or distant Northern land;
Where the gilt Chariot never marks the way,
Where none learn *Ombre*, none e'er taste *Bohea!*
There kept my charms conceal'd from mortal eye,
Like roses, that in desarts bloom and die.
What mov'd my mind with youthful Lords to roam?
160   O had I stay'd, and said my pray'rs at home!
'Twas this, the morning omens seem'd to tell;
Thrice from my trembling hand the patch-box fell;
The tott'ring China shook without a wind,
Nay *Poll* sat mute, and *Shock* was most unkind!
A *Sylph* too warn'd me of the threats of fate,
In mystic visions, now believ'd too late!
See the poor remnants of these slighted hairs!
My hands shall rend what ev'n thy rapine spares:
These, in two sable ringlets taught to break,
170   Once gave new beauties to the snowy neck;
The sister-lock now sits uncouth, alone,
And in its fellow's fate foresees its own;
Uncurl'd it hangs, the fatal sheers demands,
And tempts once more thy sacrilegious hands.
Oh hadst thou, cruel! been content to seize
Hairs less in sight, or any hairs but these!

Canto V

She said: the pitying audience melt in tears.
But Fate and *Jove* had stopp'd the Baron's ears.
In vain *Thalestris* with reproach assails,
For who can move when fair *Belinda* fails?
Not half so fix'd the *Trojan* could remain,
While *Anna* begg'd and *Dido* rag'd in vain.
Then grave *Clarissa* graceful wav'd her fan;
Silence ensu'd, and thus the nymph began.
  Say why are Beauties prais'd and honour'd most,
10 The wise man's passion, and the vain man's toast?
Why deck'd with all that land and sea afford,
Why Angels call'd, and Angel-like ador'd?
Why round our coaches crowd the white-glov'd Beaus,
Why bows the side-box from its inmost rows?
How vain are all these glories, all our pains,
Unless good sense preserve what beauty gains:
That men may say when we the front-box grace,
Behold the first in virtue, as in face!
Oh! if to dance all night, and dress all day,
20 Charm'd the small-pox, or chas'd old-age away;
Who would not scorn what housewife's cares produce,
Or who would learn one earthly thing of use?
To patch, nay ogle, might become a Saint,
Nor could it sure be such a sin to paint.
But since, alas! frail beauty must decay,
Curl'd or uncurl'd, since Locks will turn to grey;
Since painted, or not painted, all shall fade,
And she who scorns a man, must die a maid;
What then remains but well our pow'r to use,
30 And keep good-humour still whate'er we lose?
And trust me, dear! good-humour can prevail,
When airs, and flights, and screams, and scolding fail.

22

Beauties in vain their pretty eyes may roll;
Charms strike the sight, but merit wins the soul.
    So spoke the Dame, but no applause ensu'd;
Belinda frown'd, *Thalestris* call'd her Prude.
To arms, to arms! the fierce *Virago* cries,
And swift as lightning to the combat flies.
All side in parties, and begin th' attack;
40 Fans clap, silks russle and tough whalebones crack;
Heroes and Heroines shouts confus'dly rise,
And base, and treble voices strike the skies.
No common weapons in their hands are found,
Like Gods they fight, nor dread a mortal wound.
    So when bold *Homer* makes the Gods engage,
And heav'nly breasts with human passions rage;
'Gainst *Pallas*, *Mars*; *Latona*, *Hermes* arms;
And all *Olympus* rings with loud alarms:
Jove's thunder roars, heav'n trembles all around;
50 Blue *Neptune* storms, the bellowing deeps resound;
Earth shakes her nodding tow'rs, the ground gives way,
And the pale ghosts start at the flash of day!
    Triumphant *Umbriel* on a sconce's height
Clap'd his glad wings, and sate to view the fight:
Prop'd on their bodkin spears, the Sprites survey
The growing combat, or assist the fray.
    While thro' the press enrag'd *Thalestris* flies,
And scatters deaths around from both her eyes,
A Beau and Witling perish'd in the throng,
60 One dy'd in metaphor, and one in song.
'O cruel nymph! a living death I bear'
Cry'd *Dapperwit*, and sunk beside his chair.
A mournful glance Sir *Fopling* upwards cast,
Those eyes are made so killing—was his last.
Thus on *Mæander's* flow'ry margin lies
Th' expiring *Swan*, and as he sings he dies.
    When bold Sir *Plume* had drawn *Clarissa* down,

Chloe stepp'd in, and kill'd him with a frown;
She smil'd to see the doughty hero slain,
70 But, at her smile, the Beau reviv'd again.
Now *Jove* suspends his golden scales in air,
Weighs the Men's wits against the Lady's hair;
The doubtful beam long nods from side to side;
At length the wits mount up, the hairs subside.
See fierce *Belinda* on the Baron flies,
With more than usual lightning in her eyes:
Nor fear'd the Chief th'unequal fight to try,
Who sought no more than on his foe to die.
But this bold Lord with manly strength endu'd,
80 She with one finger and a thumb subdu'd:
Just where the breath of life his nostrils drew,
A charge of Snuff the wily virgin threw;
The *Gnomes* direct, to ev'ry atome just,
The pungent grains of titillating dust.
Sudden, with starting tears each eye o'erflows,
And the high dome re-echoes to his nose.
Now meet thy fate, incens'd *Belinda* cry'd,
And drew a deadly bodkin from her side.
(The same, his ancient personage to deck,
90 Her great great grandsire wore about his neck,
In three seal-rings; which after, melted down,
Form'd a vast buckle for his widow's gown:
Her infant grandame's whistle next it grew,
The bells she jingled, and the whistle blew;
Then in a bodkin grac'd her mother's hairs,
Which long she wore, and now *Belinda* wears.)
Boast not my fall (he cry'd) insulting foe!
Thou by some other shalt be laid as low,
Nor think, to die dejects my lofty mind:
100 All that I dread is leaving you behind!
Rather than so, ah let me still survive,
And burn in *Cupid's* flames,—but burn alive.

24

Restore the Lock! she cries; and all around
Restore the Lock! the vaulted roofs rebound.
Not fierce *Othello* in so loud a strain
Roar'd for the handkerchief that caus'd his pain.
But see how oft ambitious aims are cross'd,
And chiefs contend 'till all the prize is lost!
The Lock, obtain'd with guilt, and kept with pain,
110 In ev'ry place is sought, but sought in vain:
With such a prize no mortal must be blest,
So heav'n decrees! with heav'n who can contest?
    Some thought it mounted to the Lunar sphere,
Since all things lost on earth are treasur'd there.
There Hero's wits are kept in pond'rous vases,
And Beau's in snuff-boxes and tweezer-cases.
There broken vows, and death-bed alms are found,
And lover's hearts with ends of ribband bound,
The courtier's promises, and sick man's pray'rs,
120 The smiles of harlots, and the tears of heirs,
Cages for gnats, and chains to yoak a flea,
Dry'd butterflies, and tomes of casuistry.
    But trust the Muse—she saw it upward rise,
Tho' mark'd by none but quick, poetic eyes:
(So *Rome*'s great founder to the heav'ns withdrew,
To *Proculus* alone confess'd in view)
A sudden Star, it shot thro' liquid air,
And drew behind a radiant trail of hair.
Not *Berenice*'s Locks first rose so bright,
130 The heav'ns bespangling with dishevel'd light,
The *Sylphs* behold it kindling as it flies,
And pleas'd pursue its progress thro' the skies.
    This the *Beau-monde* shall from the Mall survey,
And hail with music its propitious ray.
This the blest Lover shall for *Venus* take,
And send up vows from *Rosamonda*'s lake.
This *Partridge* soon shall view in cloudless skies,

25

telescope

When next he looks thro' *Galilæo's* eyes;
And hence th'egregious wizard shall foredoom
140   The fate of *Louis*, and the fall of *Rome*. *collapse*

Then cease, bright Nymph! to mourn thy ravish'd hair,
Which adds new glory to the shining sphere!
Not all the tresses that fair head can boast,
Shall draw such envy as the Lock you lost.
For, after all the murders of your eye,
When, after millions slain, yourself shall die;
When those fair suns shall set, as set they must,
And all those tresses shall be laid in dust;
This Lock, the Muse shall consecrate to fame,
150   And 'midst the stars inscribe *Belinda's* name.

*specific ellegy –
death is a reveller, brings
us all back to the
alive. To bring us to
the truth.*

*plain speaks.
End of an
era, end of a
life.*

Notes

presentation to the class:
to find a heroic poem, to find an extract of
no less than 20 lines, compare it to
extract in ROTL in order to understand
classical allusions.

so we can understand satire.   ovids
                                 virgil.

in each canto - find 10 quotations.

Canto I

Lines 1–12

Pope imitates the customary style of an epic by first proposing his subject and then praying for inspiration. But by line 3 he has already turned the convention on its head. (See p. 76 in *Approaches*.) In these opening lines the mock-heroic tone is exhibited, but is it clear what is being mocked? What is the effect of elevating the quarrel between the Fermors and Petres into *mighty contests* while calling the loss of a curl a *trivial thing*? Is Pope using the mock-heroic style to make a jest of the occasion of the poem or does the high style of the epic opening, with its inverted syntax and declamatory tone, lend dignity to a subject which Pope calls *Slight*?

3 **Caryll, Muse** John Caryll, a Roman Catholic and dear friend to Pope, knew both families concerned in the incident. He had been guardian to Lord Petre. The *Muse* was the Goddess of poetry, one of the nine sister-goddesses who inspired the sciences and the arts. Although Pope's dedication to a human carries the joking implication that his subject may be insufficiently grand to require heavenly assistance, in all sincerity much was due to Caryll.

4 **ev'n *Belinda*** is the tone one of flattery or mockery? The word *ev'n* could be Pope laughing at Belinda's lack of interest in reading poetry (unless addressed to her personally) or he could be paying her a compliment which, although extravagant, is genuine.

6 **lays** poems. The word originally referred to poems which were sung. It was believed in the Eighteenth century that Homer and Virgil had sung their epics. Pope echoes Virgil's famous opening line in the *Aeneid*, *Arms and the Man I sing*, by claiming that he too is singing this poem.

7–8 Pope's wide-eyed claim that he cannot understand what attracts a man to a woman is a knowing joke he expects the reader to share. The word *compel* raised questions from the start. John Dennis, one of Pope's severest critics, objected at the time that it *supposes the Baron to be a Beast, not a free agent.* What difference would it make if Pope had written 'induce' or 'provoke'? The hint of compulsion may be a tribute to the power of female beauty; equally it may be trying to excuse the male advance. The same question of who is being blamed arises with the word *assault.* To what extent are the military and sexual connotations of the word brought into play? Pope may be using the word to point the narrative forward to the battle that forms the climax of the plot or it could be a sexual metaphor. The feeling of the word is aggressive, implying danger. How far is this softened by the phrase *well-bred,* suggesting that what has happened is merely a breach of polite behaviour?

8   **Belle** a pretty young woman. Belles and beaux (handsomely dressed young men) were terms commonly used in the late Seventeenth and Eighteenth centuries to refer to the fashionable young set.

9   **unexplor'd** undiscovered.

9–12   Is the irony at the expense of men or women or both? *Little men* is a mock-heroic joke, ironically contrasting contemporary male endeavours with what an epic hero would perform in *tasks so bold.* The tone of the phrase *stranger cause* raises questions. Is it teasing and affectionate or is there a sharper note, implying that any girl would be delighted to catch a lord and unlikely to refuse his advances?

Lines 13–120

The action of the poem runs through the space of a single day, a day defined by the heroine. It starts late with Belinda's noon awakening and ends at night under the light of a newly-created star. Belinda's guardian sylph, Ariel, (not named until [106]) instructs her in a dream about the unseen *bright Inhabitants of Air* [28], who accompany and protect women. In his introductory letter to Arabella Fermor in the 1714 edition, Pope claimed that he took the idea for these elemental sprites from a light-weight romantic book, *Le Comte de Gabalis*, based on the philosophical theories of the Rosicrucians, a minor seventeenth-century semi-religious, semi-philosophical society. He added freely from fairy tale and superstition (*all the Nurse and all the Priest have taught* [30]).

The sylphs are Pope's substitute for the Gods in an epic who control the fortunes of the hero and direct the outcome of events. As he did not introduce them until he expanded *The Rape* in 1714, and as he chose not to alter the narrative line, it was not possible for the sylphs to influence the action of the poem. The mock-epic joke is precisely how little real effect they have upon events. See Approaches pp. 83–4 for further discussion.

Yet they are not without influence. Their affinity with the heroine is strong whether they are seen as images of her beauty and frivolous behaviour or as leading Belinda in the direction she wishes to go. She readily accepts the command, *thy own importance know* [35] and this is the beginning both of her transformation to the status of a Goddess and of her descent into self-inflated pride. (See Approaches p. 93–4.)

13   *Sol* the sun **...** **white curtains** probably the hangings around Belinda's four-poster bed rather than at the window.

13–14   In the 1712 *Rape* these lines read: *Sol thro' white Curtains did his Beams display/And op'd those Eyes which brighter shine than they.* Pope uses a standard literary cliché to praise Belinda's eyes, i.e. they shine more brightly than the sun. You might like to consider the differences between the two versions. Does the introduction of the phrases *tim'rous ray* and *must eclipse* sharpen a conventional image or has Pope altered our perception of the heroine? (For a further consideration of the sun image see Approaches pp.104–5).

15–16   The couplet makes two apparently unrelated statements but if lovers and lap-dogs wake at the same moment is some sort of parallel, however ludicrous, suggested?

17   When Betty fails to answer the summons, Belinda impatiently knocks her slipper on the floor. The rhythm of the line echoes her irritation, with the caesura creating a pause in the middle before the quicker second half.

18   **press'd watch** the watch which she presses is a 'repeater', a fashionable and expensive type of watch made in London, which chimed to the nearest hour and quarters.

23   **Birth-night Beau** the festival held at Court on the evening of a Royal Birthday was called a Birth-night. Beaux would take pleasure in being glitteringly well-dressed for the occasion.

24   What causes Belinda to blush? There is no hint in the text. Pope, as so often in the poem, leaves it to our imaginations. Belinda herself is absolved of conscious awareness. After all, she blushes in a dream.

25   What meaning should be taken from *winning*? In the sense of the phrase 'winning ways' it means appealing or charming, a description of the surface attraction of the sylph Ariel. Is there a suggestion of another meaning, winning in the sense of gaining admission to the bedroom, to Belinda's bedside while she sleeps? If so, who is winning and what is won? Notice that Pope starts the line with the word *Seem'd*, distancing himself. As so often with the innuendos, he disclaims authorial responsibility for the suggestive pictures he creates.

29   **infant thought** the first of several instances in which Belinda is likened to a child. Refer also to lines 31–32 and 37–40 and 89.

32   **silver token** silver coin. The belief that fairies leave gifts of money continues today. When children lose their baby teeth they often put them under the pillow at night, hoping to find in the morning that they have been exchanged for money. **... circled green** rings on the lawn supposedly made by fairies dancing in a circle.

33–34   These lines illustrate the Priest's teaching as the preceding couplet did the Nurse's. They refer to the Annunciation and the ways in which virgin saints were pictured.

35   **thy own importance know** 'know thyself' was the inscription at the Delphic Oracle, the shrine dedicated to Apollo at Delphi in Greece. The Oracle's answers were held by the ancient Greeks to be of great authority but were often very ambiguous. Ariel's advice neatly echoes and subverts this piece of wisdom. Is he encouraging Belinda to a just sense of her own worth or misleading her into the sin of Pride? The question of the importance of Belinda lies at the heart of the

poem. How do you feel Pope judges her worth by the end of the poem?

37–40   These lines, together with those mentioned in the note on line 29, suggest that a quality of childishness is essential for the sylphs' protection to prevail. It allows us to see Belinda as either blamelessly innocent or childishly immature.

39   **Wits** witty, showy, young men-about-town. See also *spark* [73]

42   **Militia** troops ... **lower sky** the space between earth and moon as distinct from the heavenly regions. Does the phrase imply the existence of a superior race of spirits who inhabit the higher etherial plane, perhaps the *wise Celestials* [77]? The idea is not pursued in the poem but Pope seems to be warning us not to take the sylphs too seriously. In spite of their airs and graces, of their claims to *contrive it all* [104], can they perform all they promise?

44   **Box ... Ring** a box at the theatre and the Ring in Hyde Park, a fashionable place around which to drive, and be seen driving, in a carriage.

45   **Equipage** a private carriage and horses with attendant servants.

46   **a Chair** sedan chair, carried by two men.

49   **transition** perhaps an early reference to an idea that runs through the poem, that women's natures are changeable.

50   **Vehicles** by using a heavy, trundling word as a metaphor for women's earthly bodies and a lighter word *Equipage* for their lives as sylphs, Ariel reinforces his claim that women move more freely and elegantly after their transformation. Is an airy existence more desirable than a human one? The choice between elegance and earthly passion is one which Belinda faces.

55–56   **Chariots ... *Ombre*** carriages were called 'chariots' at the time. *Ombre* is a card game, and is the game which Belinda and the Baron play in Canto III. Behind these *vanities* lies the echo of epic times when chariots carried heroes into battle and games were contests of physical prowess.

59–66   The four types of sprite which Ariel describes are based on the medieval belief that our physical bodies consisted of four base elements; air, fire, earth and water, and that human character was formed by whichever element predominated. For example, the spirits of fiery women are associated with salamanders, mythological reptilian creatures who, it was believed, could live in fire. Salamanders and nymphs disappear quickly from the poem; gnomes are reserved for the Cave of Spleen. Ariel's explanation concentrates upon the sylphs.

59 **Termagants** angry, scolding women, i.e. fiery.

62 **Tea** in the Eighteenth century *tea* rhymed with *away*.

65 **Coquettes** young flirtatious women.

68 **embrac'd** taken in charge, protected. The offer of the sylph's embrace as a reward for remaining chaste, and the manner in which the structure of the couplet closely associates the alternatives, may hint at sexual undertones. If so, the following couplet could re-establish the innocence of the sylphs by stressing their disembodied natures. Or, bearing in mind how Jupiter, King of the Gods, transformed himself into different shapes in order to seduce mortals, it could be read as a vision of limitless pleasure. The lightness of tone (consider the cumulative effect of *sport and flutter*; *freed from mortal laws, with ease assume; what shapes they please*) seems delicately to keep these possibilities both open and unresolved.

72 **masquerades** masked assemblies and balls.

73 **spark** witty, gay, young man.

78 ***Honour*** this is the first mention of the word which becomes so significant as the poem develops. For a discussion of what the sylphs might intend by the term, see Approaches pp. 85–7

79 **too conscious of their face** too aware of their beauty.

81 **prospects** expectations of a titled marriage.

89 **bidden blush** a 'blush' created by make-up.

91–104 To describe the world of women as *mystic mazes* and a *giddy circle* of *vanities*, suggests that Pope considers women have no sense of purpose or direction. Yet he also refers to them as *tender* and *victim*. Is his attitude to their changeable natures critical or sympathetic? And if you feel that it is the latter, does this carry with it an element of patronage? (See Approaches pp. 95–6.)

92 **mystic** although the adjective properly describes the mazes, is there a sense that the ways of women are mysterious to men? See also line 122.

94   **impertinence** silliness, foolishness, nonsense.

97–98   **Florio ... Damon** standard literary names for lovers in light verse.

100   **Toyshop** on the one hand the image asserts the essential instability and frivolity of women. (In the Eighteenth century *Toyshop* referred to a shop selling trinkets, knick-knacks and fancy goods for adults.) On the other, it reveals the powerlessness of the sylphs who *shift* a heart which is already *moving*.

101   **sword-knots** braided cord fastened to the handles of swords allowing the wearer to twist the cord around his wrist for security.

105   I, who claim to protect you, am one of these (sylphs). Pope's inverted syntax emphasizes Ariel's boast.

109   **impend** approach.

110   **main** the open ocean.

118–119   **Billet-doux ...** love letter. **Wounds, Charms, and Ardors ...** the language of eighteenth-century romantic flattery.

120   Visions and warning dreams are customary in epics and customarily vanish, but there may be a hint that the vision is lost because of Belinda's empty-headed nature. See also note on lines 91–104 above.

Lines 121–148

In a parody of the ritual of epic heroes arming for battle, Betty helps to dress Belinda for an evening of coffee and cards at Hampton Court. In the epic world this preparation often led to death. Pope adopts the phraseology and solemn tone of the epic (*Now awful Beauty puts on all its arms* [139]). Does some sense of the gravity of the epic moment come across in these lines in spite of the diminishing nature of the parallel with a young girl making-up?

The tone of the first bedroom scene, Belinda's awakening, is mocking and suggestive. The blushes, the drowsiness, the impatience, the ease with which she is distracted and flattered by the conventional phrases of a billet-doux; all these make her appear very young and human. In this passage the narrator's attitude changes from one of amused indulgence to one of adoration. We are witnesses to the transformation of Belinda from an innocent girl to a Goddess. (See Approaches pp. 92–4.) As well as echoing epic phrases, Pope uses religious imagery to create a tone which is awed and reverential, raising questions about the degree to which he is genuinely mocking. Worshipped and *deck'd with all that land and sea afford* [V 11] Belinda *arms herself* … for what? The question hangs in the air and like so many questions in the poem (*what strange motive … Was it for this you took such constant care?*) it is left hanging.

125–126   In *Paradise Lost* the newly created Eve glimpsed herself in a pool of water and fell in love with her image before she had set eyes on Adam or understood about reflections. Pope's allusion contrasts Milton's scene of pre-fallen innocence with Belinda's worship of her own reflection. However *heav'nly*, she knows full well whose image she sees in the mirror.

127   **inferior Priestess** Betty. The superior Priestess is Belinda who worships her own image in the glass.

131   **nicely culls with curious toil** selects precisely with attentive concentration.

132   **spoil** plunder, booty, valuables seized in war. Dryden used the phrase *glitt'ring spoil* in his translation of the *Aeneid* to describe armour which had been captured in battle. In the toilette *spoil* is reduced to jewellery and perfume. These are Belinda's *arms* [139], seductive weapons for the battleground of Hampton Court. However, the word *spoil* could suggest that the arms were acquired in a suspect, unearned manner. (For a further discussion see Approaches p. 83.)

135–136   **Tortoise … Elephant** Belinda's combs of *speckled* tortoise-shell and *white* ivory are examples of the idea of transformation which runs through the poem. (See Approaches p. 96–7.)

138   **Patches, Bibles** patches of black material were worn by women on their faces as fashionable beauty marks. Small editions of *Bibles*, no more than a few inches in width or

length and elegantly bound, were produced in the Eighteenth century for ladies to carry.

This famous line has been variously interpreted. Some critics feel that the word *Bibles* is incongruously slipped into the confusion of make-up and love letters to reveal the frivolous nature of Belinda's mind, unable to distinguish between things of lasting worth and things of the moment. Others have viewed the confusion of her dressing table as an imaginative profusion from which she arises, a newly-created Goddess. Critics who stress the economic basis of her adornment point to the resemblance between this line and mercantile lists of the Eighteenth century which listed luxury objects indiscriminately. Products appeared in these catalogues because of their market value, not their moral worth. Then there is the question of the plurals. The likelihood is that the bibles are tiny. Could this be an accurate description of a young girl's dressing table with several elegantly small bibles lying there? What of the tone set by the alliteration and the movement from monosyllable to disyllables and a closing trisyllable? The way in which we read the line depends ultimately upon the way in which we view Belinda.

139   **awful** creating awe. The long vowels *awe ... all ... arms* have a solemn sound. Do they suggest danger, a hint that Belinda's beauty may be a weapon in a battle yet to come? Or do you feel that they create a sense that Pope is in awe of the transformed Belinda?

143   **purer blush** why should a blush applied by rouge be purer? The *bidden blush* [89] seemed to suggest a loss of innocence in *Infant cheeks*. Here Pope appears to favour a more sophisticated and refined beauty. Is he, as some critics have thought, falling in love with an artificial beauty he intended to mock?

143   **keener lightnings** some form of eyedrop has been applied, perhaps belladonna which enlarged the pupils.

148   Notice how the tone which has remained grave, almost awed, throughout the passage is neatly undercut by the joke in the concluding line which returns us sharply from the altar to the boudoir. Pope apparently wants us to go out smiling.

Canto II

Lines 1–28

The verse paragraphs read like a swelling paean of praise to Belinda who *issues forth* from her toilette, transformed into a goddess rivalling the sun. Everything shines: the Thames, the nymphs and youths, her cross, her eyes and her ringlets. Surrounded by lesser luminaries as the sun is surrounded by comets, she is the undoubted centre of attraction. *But ev'ry eye was fix'd on her alone* [6]. However, the word *But* which opens the line suggests that not all is quite as it should be. The couplets recoil upon themselves, hinting alternative readings. The mention of Jews and Infidels throws doubt on the religious significance of the *sparkling Cross*, which is worn presumably for ornamentation not devotion, and chosen to display wealth and beauty not faith. One of the best examples of Pope's skill at undercutting the apparent claims of his couplets is the presence of the word *unfix'd* in line 10. It returns the reader to line 9 and Belinda's *sprightly mind*. Are we to take *sprightly* as a compliment or not? In the sense of 'lively' it appears to praise Belinda but allied to *unfix'd* it implies that her attention darts from one thing to another in a shallow, scatty manner. (And what of the contrast with *fix'd* in line 6 to describe the devotion of her admirers?) As Pope's balanced couplets spring forward and turn back on themselves, one wonders whether to trust his first line or look for twists in the tail. How sincere, for example, do you find line 18?

2   **main** ocean.
3   **the rival of his beams** this is not the first time that Belinda has been compared favourably to the sun. (For a discussion of the sun image throughout the poem see Approaches pp. 104–5.)

7–8   The cross may serve to decorate the real object of adoration; *kiss* suggestively draws attention to her *white breast*.

11–12   Notice the antithesis of *none ... all*; *Oft ... never*. Do the words balance or cancel each other? You may feel they create a sense of a poised Belinda, smoothing over any possible offence with her smiles. On the other hand you might ask whether a smile is worth the favour she refuses to give.

14   **alike** another of those little twists at the end of the couplet which undermine the sense of what has gone before. Are we to take Belinda's liberality as evidence of her generosity of spirit or of her self-absorption?

15–18   **Yet ... If** the syntax insists upon indecisiveness, balancing between admiration and mockery. See also *But* in line 6.

25   **sprindges** snares for catching birds.

26   In Pope's time fishing lines were made of horse-hair. *Finny prey* is an example of what Pope called a diminishing figure. (See Approaches pp. 99–100.) The ordinariness of the thing described, fish, is concealed by pompous language which indicates a lack of proportion in the poet's choice of words. The joke is created partly by the inappropriate use of language and partly by the sense that the characters in the poem are taking themselves over-seriously.

Lines 29–46

At this, our first encounter with the Baron, what portrait are we given? The syntax of lines 30–31, unencumbered with adjectives or adverbs, and the rapidity with which the three verbs in line 30 follow each other, fit the image of a decisive *advent'rous* man, but *force ... ravish ...* and *fraud* [32] disturb this idea. What image of manliness is presented here if the Baron's battle honours are *trophies of his former loves*? Is he regarding Belinda as merely another trophy? (Note the hunting as well as military connotations of the word.) It is difficult not to sense ridicule in Pope's description of his ardent prayers. (See Approaches p. 78.) Is this in any way softened by the verbs in lines 35–43 and the phrases *tender Billet-doux* and *empty air*?

29 **Baron** no other character in the poem fails to be accorded the dignity (or intimacy) of a personal name.

35 *Phoebus* the sun.

41 **pyre** a pile of wood or combustible material, usually a funeral pile for burning a dead body.

45–46 These lines allude to incidents in the *Iliad* and *Aeneid*. Gods commonly granted only half the hero's prayer.

Lines 47–142

In these lines we have our first detailed picture of the sylphs and their contradictory natures, at one and the same time both colourful and nearly invisible. Their glittering appearances are vivid and elusive as their *fluid bodies* and *transparent forms* rapidly change and dissolve. Verbs of motion crowd lines 47–72. Many are intransitive, taking no object, perhaps suggesting that the restless movements reflect back upon the sylphs themselves. It is their own shapes and forms which are changed by this activity. Does it hint at a further idea, that their actions have little effect on anyone in the poem but themselves? (For a fuller discussion of the theme of change within the poem see Approaches pp. 96–7.)

Like the Greek and Roman Gods, the sylphs descend from their airy, upper world to intervene in the human sphere, adding to the poem that sense of the 'marvellous' which eighteenth-century readers expected in an epic, a sense that human destinies are ultimately controlled by supernatural forces who can arrange visions and visitations, appearances and disappearances, failures and victories with magical, divine power. By the addition of the sylphs (or 'machinery' as the supernatural element in an epic was known), Pope's protagonists lead their lives under the watchful care of divine beings. The difference with the mock-epic is that, for all their pretensions to power, the sylphs are powerless to control the action of the poem.

Notice how the military imagery which was introduced in Canto I, with *the light Militia of the lower sky* [42], continues in these lines. The *lucid squadrons* are commanded by a superior *chief* who exhorts them as before a battle, orders out a *special* patrol to guard the enemy's objective and punishes them for disobeying orders, *Whatever spirit, careless of his charge/His post neglects ... Shall feel sharp vengeance* [123–125]. The sylphs are warriors in Belinda's defence. The joke is that their willingness to defend may exceed Belinda's desire to be defended.

47   **secure** safely.

51   **Zephyrs** gentle winds. Zephyr was the classical Greek God of the west wind.

52   Belinda's smiles are associated with the warming and life-giving properties of the sun. Perhaps no other line in the poem so forcefully claims divine powers for her.

55–57   Notice the sibilants in these lines. They sound like the swish of silk or the feathering of wings.

55   **Denizens** inhabitants. In its literal sense, denizens refers to aliens who have been granted citizenship. Perhaps this is a glancing reference to the sylphs' previous existence on earth.

57   **shrouds** literally the ropes which haul the sails, but here the sails themselves.

70   **Superior** Satan in *Paradise Lost* is called *the superior Fiend* [Bk 1 283] in the sense of being the most exalted, the most important, which also applies here. Ariel is the *chief*, whom the aerial band must obey [73]. The epic hero was naturally taller than his comrades. Ariel however owes his elevated position not to his physical stature, as did Satan or Achilles, but to his being perched on the mast-head.

73–90   Ariel addresses the band of sylphs with names which, taken from *Le Comte de Gabalis*, appear only at this point in the poem. Does this give you the sense of an innumerable band of troops ready to defend Belinda? Or does the roll-call of duties, on a cosmic scale and culminating in the defence of the British Throne, mock the more trivial duties of the sylphs assigned to Belinda in lines 91–100?

77   **Æther** the purest aerial region, above the moon.

79   **wand'ring orbs** comets.

81   **less refin'd** the region between the earth and the moon, which was not considered as pure in nature as the celestial regions beyond the moon's influence.

86   **glebe** cultivated land; fields of corn.

88–90   The key commands *Watch … guide … guard* are placed at the climax of the verse paragraph. (For further discussion of the sylphs' duties see Approaches pp. 84–5.)

91   **humbler province** after describing the celestial duties assigned to angels, *th'aerial kind*, Ariel comes to the significantly humbler tasks of the sylphs.

92   **pleasing … glorious** the apposition of the two adjectives suggests that one excludes the other. This may look forward to the ending when Belinda's lock, transformed to a comet in the celestial regions, *adds new glory to the shining sphere!* [V 142]. Belinda could be said to achieve glory at the cost of suffering personal displeasure. Yet the tone of the poem accords more with the first adjective than the second.

95   **vernal** spring.

97   **wash** cosmetic lotion.

100   **Flounce … Furbelow** material gathered or pleated to form borders for petticoats and dresses.

103   **slight** trickery. The line echoes the Baron's determination to win the lock by *force* or *fraud* [II 32].

105–110   These lines have been interpreted in various ways. Some readers find Pope's teasing of Belinda and the disasters which threaten her sympathetic and affectionate while others think he is being ironically critical. Ariel predicts a series of *dire* events in a balanced set of clauses which juxtapose the serious and the trivial in a ludicrous mixture. For Belinda to lose her virginity is surely a *dire disaster*, yet the balanced syntax of the closing line of the couplet, placing the noun prominently before its verb, implies that the sylphs value the China jar even more. In the following couplets, one verb yokes together events of incomparably different degrees of importance. Ariel's confused morality in which virtue lies in unflawed appearances is mockingly revealed and the lightness of tone suggests that Belinda shares the sylphs' excessive concern with outward show. (See Approaches pp. 100–101 and pp. 84–5 for further discussion.)

105   *Diana* Goddess of the moon, of hunting and chastity. Breaking *Diana's law* meant to lose one's virginity.

110   Not for the first time there is a suggestion that Belinda's heart belongs more to her lap-dog than to a man. It may be that the

fall of Shock, so plaintively predicted here, occurs during the game of cards.

111–115   The sylphs' names derive from their duties. Zephyretta echoes Zephyr, the gentle west wind; Brillante the look of jewelled ear drops; Momentilla belongs to moments of time and Crispissa to the crisping of locks. Does the sound of their names convey a sense of their sylph-like qualities?

114   Belinda presumably wears her repeater watch hanging from her waist which was the fashion of the times.

116   The importance of Shock is stressed. Ariel assumes personal protection of him. See Approaches pp. 103–4 for a discussion of the relationship between lap-dogs and lovers.

117   The fifty sylphs of *special note* are not mentioned again in the poem. Perhaps Pope highlights them to create a rhyme which throws *Petticoat* into prominence, for what is special is the petticoat itself. It is the citadel under attack and its close proximity hints that it is a symbol of her honour and a metaphor for her chastity.

118   **Petticoat** the fashion of the time was to wear a lower garment which was visible. Over it Belinda would have worn a loose dress or coat pinned back in front to reveal the 'petticoat'. See illustration on p. 117.

119   **seven-fold fence** the 'folds' are the layers of leather from which a Greek shield was made. Epic heroes customarily had shields fashioned from seven layers of leather. Achilles' shield was specially made for him by the God Vulcan who bound it with silver around the circumference. It was so famous that eighteenth-century readers would have had no difficulty in recognizing the allusion to it in Belinda's petticoat.

120   **hoops ... whale** Belinda's petticoat is hooped and stiffened with whalebone.

121–122   Notice how the military metaphors delicately insinuate the underlying cause of the battle. As with the lock, Pope leaves the reader to decide the extent to which the Baron seeks articles of adornment for trophies and the extent to which they act as metaphors.

123–136   Given the sylphs' concern with appearances it seems fitting that their punishments should also lie in this field and that the instruments of restraint should be the very things they use as beauty aids when adorning Belinda. You might like to compare this passage with the scene in which Belinda applies her make-up [I 139–146]. Notice how Pope's choice of words presents the same event in two different lights, the first a divine transformation; the second a torture chamber. The diminutive size of the sylphs and their desire to remain always on the wing is turned against them, amusingly so, if one visualizes the bodkin's eye and seas of frothing chocolate which read like illustrations of a child's nursery book. Yet the language alludes to both Greek and Christian mythology; to Ixion and to Miltons' Lucifer who had his flight restrained, imparting a note of grandeur to the mess of make-up and beauty aids. The verbs which limit their restless movement: *stop'd, transfix'd, plung'd, wedg'd, restrain, clog'd*, reveal however another side to the ritual of make-up. The application of cosmetics was probably quite painful and some beauty aids, like those which contained white lead, were dangerous to health. The effort required to keep up appearances which is hinted at here will be developed more fully by Thalestris in Canto V.

126   **vials** small glass bottles.

128   **bodkin** a small tool made of metal or bone, usually, as in this line, a blunt-headed needle. The bodkin in Canto V with which Belinda attacks the Baron is a decorative pin fastening her dress and previously worn by her mother as a hairpin.

129   **Pomatums** scented ointments applied to the skin or hair.

131   **Alom stypticks** Alum is an astringent white mineral salt. *Stypticks* are substances which contract body tissue.

132   **rivell'd** contracted into wrinkles.

133   *Ixion* in Greek mythology, Ixion attempted to seduce Hera, the Queen of the Gods. Zeus, King of the Gods, forestalled and punished him by binding him to a fiery wheel which rolled unceasingly through the skies.

134   **Mill** chocolate, a fashionable drink at this time especially for women, was made by grinding cacao nuts and infusing the powder with hot water. The *whirling Mill* refers to the chocolate pot in which the powder was infused. A swizzle stick fitted into the pot through a hole in the lid and was rotated between the palms until the drink frothed.

139   **thrid** thread.

Canto III

Lines 1–24

The description of Hampton Court opens in epic style taking its
syntax and vocabulary from Dryden's translation of the *Aeneid*
and in particular from a passage about the walls of Carthage. For
how long is the grand style maintained? By lines 9–18 are we not
in the linguistic world of eighteenth-century society, where
nymphs and heroes *taste* the *pleasures of a Court*? Pope's colloquial
and all that has an easy, careless air. It is a lazy phrase which fits
the indolent world of the beau monde. Perhaps the descent from
high style starts with the use of zeugma in lines 6 and 8. (See
Approaches pp. 102–3.) Does the suggestion that the fall of
tyrants and the fall of nymphs are of equal concern to *Britain's
statesmen* mock the gravity of the scene so grandiloquently set
forth in the first lines or does it lend gravity to the 'fall' of nymphs
and to Belinda's situation?

    1   **meads** meadows.

   3–4 The palace at Hampton Court, built by Cardinal Wolsey in
        the Sixteenth century and extended by Sir Christopher Wren
        in the Seventeenth, was Queen Anne's favourite royal
        residence. It lay on the banks of the Thames, a few miles
        upstream from the City of London. The condition of the
        roads in the early Eighteenth century meant that travel by the
        river was preferable as well as pleasant.

    7   **three realms** England, Ireland and Scotland.

    8   A famous example of Pope's use of zeugma (See Approaches
        p. 102.) in which a single verb takes two grammatically
        correct but stylistically incongruous objects. In the space of a
        single line the tone shifts abruptly and comically from the
        stately epic to the voice of a wit-about-town.

   12   **visit** a evening social visit. (See also the note on line
        167.)

14   ***Indian* screen** used to shield the direct heat of the fire and probably made of lacquer. At this time India and Arabia referred generally to the East. The screen could be from Japan.

19–24   This is one of the few moments in the poem when the daily life of the City openly surfaces and these famous lines have been variously interpreted. They are based upon a standard epic device for indicating that the time is evening by reference to labourers ceasing their daily work, but many readers have felt a cutting edge in the close of the couplet formed by lines 21 and 22. Pope's implication, that lives are being sacrificed for convenience, may horrify and could be taken as a serious criticism of the rituals of etiquette. The tone, however, is so elegantly mocking that one does not know whether to read the lines as unserious teasing or bitter satire.

23   ***Exchange*** in the Eighteenth century businessmen did not work in offices as they do today. They transacted their affairs at coffee shops, many of which became associated with a particular branch of business, or at the Royal Exchange which was a two-storey building in the City, a few streets to the north of London Bridge. It had arcades around an open courtyard where men gathered to do to business with each other. (See p. 117 for illustration.)

Lines 25–100

The epic allusions are to sports contests where warriors competed at athletics and practised their battle skills, rather than to a battle. The imitation of an epic battle is delayed until Canto V, but do you feel a sense of a preliminary skirmish in these lines; a hint that the game of cards is either a screen or a metaphor for a sexual contest? The Baron's feelings are not disclosed. We see the game from Belinda's point of view and the language suggests a rising passion; *Burns to encounter, swells her breast,* but it is unclear to what extent she is aware of this herself. Is she innocent, naïvely flirtatious or aflame with desire?

26 **advent'rous Knights** the Baron was introduced as *advent'rous* [II 29]. *Knights* may refer simply to the titled rank of Belinda's opponents but the word is suggestive of medieval tournaments with their air of mock battles. (See also the note on line 129) Is there also a pun intended, hinting a different kind of adventure?

27 ***Ombre*** a popular card game in Pope's time. It came originally from Spain (the name derives from the Spanish word *Hombre*, meaning 'man') and bears a resemblance to our contemporary game of whist. Nine rounds are played and to win a player needs to gain a majority of rounds or tricks. The third Knight is a necessary but shadowy character. Sometimes it is impossible to tell what cards he holds or plays. The contest is entirely between Belinda and the Baron. She must win five tricks to his four if she is to be the victor.

28 The suggestive phrase *swells her breast* implies that her *conquests* may not be merely at cards.

29–30 Each of the three players is dealt nine cards which make up the *three bands* of opposing warriors *in arms*. In spite of the epic allusion being to games on the sports field, the military metaphor is sustained throughout the contest, perhaps conveying a sense that not all the players are treating the game merely as a pastime. The *sacred nine* refers both to the number of cards each player holds and to the Muses, the sister-goddesses of arts and learning.

33 **Matadore** the aces, plus one other card depending upon which suit was chosen for trump.

37–38 Does the quirky, humorous quality of this couplet owe something to the odd alliteration, *four Kings … forky*?

41 **garbs succinct** short tunics.

42 **halberts** weapons which combined a spear and battle-axe on the same shaft.

44 **velvet plain** a phrase commonly used in pastoral and epic poetry to describe a green field. It refers here to the velvet-covered card table, but there may also be a sense of the plain or field of battle.

46 The line parodies the Biblical phrase. *And God said, 'Let there be light' and there was light* [Genesis i 3]. Although there is a ludicrous imbalance in comparing God creating light out of darkness on the first day of creation with a young girl

declaring trumps in a game of cards, the comparison adds to the sense that, within the world of the poem, Belinda is a Goddess. In one sense it shows the ridiculous heights to which pride has brought her, and sets her up for a fall. In another sense it continues the image which runs through the poem of Belinda as the sun, the light of the world upon which not only the Baron but all the *gazers* depend. *Belinda smil'd, and all the world was gay* [II 52].

47–48   **sable ... swarthy** Belinda opens the game leading spades and clubs.

49   *Spadillio* Ace of Spades.

51   *Manillio* two of Spades.

53   *Basto* Ace of Clubs.

61   *Pam* Knave of Clubs.

62   *Lu* Lu or Loo is the name of a different card game in which the Knave of Clubs is the most powerful card.

67   *Amazon* the Queen of Spades. In Greek mythology the Amazons were a tribe of warrior women.

69   Her first victim to die is the King of Clubs. The reversed syntax imitates the epic style.

70   **mien** features, expression.

71   **What boots** what helps.

76   **embroider'd** a common epic adjective. There is no sense intended of a piece of embroidery.

77   **refulgent** shining, gleaming.

80   **strow** strew.

87–92   Belinda's early success, easily winning four tricks in a row, appeared to put her in a unbeatable position. She needed only one more trick to win the game outright, and this is called *Codille*. However the Baron wrested back the lead and took the fifth to eighth tricks. The game now stands at four tricks each. Everything depends upon who wins the final hand and Belinda *trembles* as she suddenly faces the prospect of losing a game which had seemed certainly hers. The sly references to the *wily* Knave and Queen of *Hearts* and the *shameful chance* at which the *virgin* blood forsakes her cheeks hint at more sensual reasons for her trembling. Hints are all we have. Pope delicately leaves the reader to judge the extent to which Belinda's passion is being aroused by the fear of losing at cards or winning at a quite different game.

96 **Trick** the Baron leads with the powerful Ace of Hearts but the winning card, the King of Hearts, is in Belinda's hand. Does any sense of trickery or cleverness on Belinda's part lie behind the surface meaning of the word *Trick*? She holds the King by luck but you may feel that *lurk'd* and *unseen* invest her playing with an air of cunning strategy. If so, does this increase for you the sense of her power or do you feel she is misled by a fortuitous win at cards into believing herself more powerful than she really is?

Lines 101–124

Epic warnings customarily told of mortal ruin and reminded heroes that their ultimate doom was certain. The lofty language and tone of lines 101–104 would not be out of place in an epic translation. Pope continues the high style in lines 105–112. Epic feasts were described in just such words in eighteenth-century translations. At what point does epic rhetoric and diction give way to the casual tone of eighteenth-century conversation? The brackets around the aside in lines 117–118 have the air of Pope nudging us and dropping a knowing remark into our ear. We are invited, by the colloquial tone, to share in court and coffee-house gossip. You may decide that phrases which point to the transition between the grandeur of the epic and the frivolity of eighteenth-century society appear even earlier. To which world do *the Fair* belong?

This passage is one of the occasions in the poem when the contrast in scale between the two worlds serves to magnify as well as ridicule and diminish. As with Belinda's toilette, the tone of grandeur and mystery created by such phrases as *crown'd . . . grateful … gratify … China's earth receives the smoaking tyde* seems to raise the act of drinking coffee to an elaborate ritual which Pope enjoys and reveres. Should readers share this admiration for the good things in life or take the lines as purely ironic? As so often, Pope seems to allow us to read the lines either way, or both at the same time.

106 Coffee berries were first roasted in a chafing dish on the sideboard (the crackling sound) and then ground in a mill. See also chocolate mills [II 134].

107 Lacquer work from Japan began arriving in England from the East during the Seventeenth century and small items of oriental lacquered furniture, such as chests, cabinets, screens and tables, were the height of fashion in Pope's time. The image of furniture as an altar at which this society worships was hinted earlier in the language Pope used to describe Belinda's toilette in Canto I. The tone here is similarly reverential. Lines 107–112 magnify the etiquette of coffee drinking into a religious ceremony (*shining Altars ... silver lamp ... fiery spirits ... silver spouts*) and the act of worship is no longer private but communal with overtones of Nature's creative power. *China's earth* (the cups) receives the *grateful* liquor. What are the implications of *grateful*? Do you think that the adjective transfers its sense to the thirsty participants or, as the grammar suggests, the *earth*? The scale of the description is ridiculously exaggerated, but do you detect irony in these lines? It may be that some sense of the preciousness and beauty of these items in the Eighteenth century and in the world of the poem pulls against the implied criticism of people who take social ceremonies so seriously. (See Approaches pp. 81–3.)

118 **half-shut eyes** The apparent compliment to a politician's wisdom (i.e. that with eyes only half opened he can see through *all things*) is undermined by the ironic alternative meaning (i.e. that his half-considered judgement is superficial and probably wrong.)

119 **vapours** clouds of steam. The word appears innocent in this line, referring to steam from the Baron's coffee. However, once we reach the *constant Vapour* [IV 39] which fills the Cave of Spleen and realize the undertones of ill-humour and disease which accompany the vapours we can recognize how deftly Pope has amalgamated the literal sense of the word with its poisonous and mischievous attributes.

122–124 In classical mythology, *Scylla* was the daughter of King *Nisus* who, amongst his silver hair, had one purple lock of magical power upon which the security of himself and his kingdom depended. Scylla fell in love with her father's enemy Minos and stole the lock to give to him. For this sacrilegious theft she was rejected by Minos and turned into a bird. Like the reference to Berenice's locks [V 129] this comparison highlights the importance of locks of hair.

Lines 125–178

Though *two-edg'd weapon* [128] is clearly part of a cluster of battle imagery describing the Baron's attack, (*stratagems* [120], *Knight* [129], *spear ... arm ... fight* [130]) it is less obvious that this phrase refers to a tiny pair of ladies' scissors. The distance in the comparison between scissors and a *spear* is ludicrously emphasized by the phrase *little engine on his fingers' ends*. The Baron is unable to fit his male fingers fully into the scissors. *Two edg'd weapon* and *glitt'ring Forfex* are further examples of periphrasis (see the note on line 26) in which the ordinariness of the object is teasingly concealed behind somewhat mysterious and elevated epic phraseology. When Pope arrives at his final epic phrase, *fatal engine*, the seriousness with which we might regard the Baron's rape of the lock is undercut by the presence of an eighteenth-century voice, redolent of gossip and light-weight tittle-tattle. *Just then* [127] ... *just behind* [133] ... *A wretched Sylph* [150].

144 **lurking** why has Belinda used *all her art* to conceal from Ariel the idea of an earthly lover in her mind or heart? By refusing the sylphs' enticements to reject mankind [I 67–68] she loses their protection. Is there a sense of guile on her part? See also the note on line 96 on *lurk'd*. If you feel that this is so, do you think that Pope wishes us to approve or disapprove of her 'fall' from the sylphs' grace?

147 **Forfex** the Latin word for scissors, a deliberately pompous choice of a word rarely used even in the Eighteenth century.

151–152 In Greek mythology, the Fates were three aged, blind goddesses who spun the thread of a man or woman's life. When the time came to end it, they cut the thread with shears. The sombre tone set by the allusion in the first line of the couplet is turned on its head by the airily dismissive tone of the concluding line. (See Approaches pp. 101–2.) Is there the slightest of warnings that, while airy substances can escape Fate, mortals are more vulnerable? If you find this is an over-serious interpretation, in danger of spoiling the joke in this couplet, it is still a point of view which appears with increasing insistence in the remainder of the poem.

157–160   The reversal of the normal word order in this sentence sets the high epic tone, a tone mockingly undercut by the juxtaposition of husbands with lap-dogs and China vessels with the lock of hair. In this confusion of emotion and morality where do Pope's sympathies lie?

164   **Coach and six** a coach and three pairs of horses.

165   *Atalantis* refers to *Secret Memoirs and Manners of Several Persons of Quality, of Both Sexes. From the New Atalantis, an Island in the Mediterranean* by Mrs Manley. This was a salacious book purporting to reveal contemporary scandals.

167–168   Evening visits, accompanied by servants bearing torches, were part of the fashionable lady's social round.

173–174   The destruction of the towers and battlements of Troy, held to have been built by the Gods, was part of the revenge of the Greeks on the Trojans at the end of their bitter ten-year siege of the city.

Canto IV

Lines 1–54

Gnome

Umbriel's visit to the Cave of Spleen is a mock allusion to another epic set piece, the descent of the hero to the underworld. The *gloomy Cave* is a *proper scene* for the Gnome Umbriel who is described variously as *sooty, dusky, melancholy* and with *black wings. The fair face of light* which his presence *sully'd* could well describe the sylphs, (do you recall the adjectives associated with them? See Approaches pp. 79–80) and the *glittering world*

contrast with underworld

which Belinda inhabits. With a smile Belinda makes her world
gay, whereas Spleen, a *wayward Queen*, lives in a *dismal dome.*
Screen'd in shades from day's detested glare, the Goddess *with a
discontented air* rules an underworld defined by contrast with
Belinda's shimmering daylight sphere; dark against light, black
against gold, sooty against gilded, gloomy against gay. [*Belinda's world against the under world*]

Pope draws also upon Ovid's *Metamorphoses* and upon a
description in that work of the gloomy cave where the Goddess
Envy dwells. The *Metamorphoses* is a collection of stories about
humans who were changed into natural forms: trees, flowers,
animals, stars. In a similar way the Cave of Spleen is a place of
transformations. Pope's description refers in lines 43–46 to the
scenic transformations of contemporary theatrical illusions and
scattered throughout the Cave are *Unnumber'd throngs* of *bodies
chang'd to various forms* [47–8]. Are we to take this perverse
transformation of everyday objects, bottles and jars and teapots,
as further proof of the ugliness of the Cave in contrast with the
beauty of the world above? Or do the strangely altered shapes
symbolize Spleen's power to transform the appearance and
behaviour of women? She is pictured as a *wayward* Goddess
served by *Ill-nature* and *Affectation*. Umbriel openly boasts of how
he helps to put women into bad-tempered moods which *spoil a
grace.*

Lines 53–54 hint at more sinister, sexual undertones to the
deformation of jars and bottles. Among the recognized symptoms
of Spleen were hallucinations and delusions. Medical treatises
described cases of patients who believed they had changed into
familiar, domestic objects. Pope in a note to the 1736 edition of
his *Works* claimed that he knew for a *real fact* a lady of distinction
who imagined she was a goosepie. Beneath the nursery-rhyme
humour of the oddity of the transformations in the Cave of
Spleen lies a sense of frustration and repression, (the *phantoms*
and *dreams* of *hermits* and *expiring maids*), of neurotic fears and
delusions breaking out in images of warped sexuality which leave
one wondering whether the passage is a compliment to Belinda or
a warning of how she too might be transformed by Spleen. (See
Approaches pp. 89–91.)

1–2   Pope drew attention in the 1736 edition of his *Works* to the opening of the *Aeneid* IV where Dido, widowed Queen of Carthage, is falling in love with Aeneas against her better judgement. Dryden's translation reads:

> *But anxious Cares already seiz'd the Queen;*
> *She fed within her Veins a Flame unseen:*

Pope's concern that readers note the epic allusion raises questions. Is Belinda's anxiety and shame over her trivial loss diminished by the comparison with Dido's dilemma, torn between the love-longings of reawakened passion and the fear of putting herself and her kingdom into the hands of a stranger? Or does the tone of his lines echo the seriousness of the original, suggesting that Belinda too may be stirred by love-longings for the Baron, the *secret passions* which, as a virgin, she is less able than Dido to understand?

3–10   The passage builds to a climax through repetition and reiteration, the syntax of parallel clauses implying a sustained increase of intensity which collapses when we reach the pettiness of Cynthia's sulks after the generalized, sweeping claims of the preceding examples. As so often in the poem, unexpected shifts in style deflate the apparent meaning of the passage. The first line of each couplet could have come from an epic translation; the second line from lightweight contemporary satiric verse against women. Each couplet has a high/low, serious/mocking, male/female contrast. Note how the male/female antithesis within the couplets sets the frustration felt when an active, epic, male impulse is blocked against the frustrations of female passivity. Consider what this implies about the opportunities available to men and women and the different codes of behaviour expected of them. (See Approaches pp. 95–6.)

4   Compare this line with Clarissa's warning, *she who scorns a man, must die a maid* [V 28]. This is not the first time that the poem has hinted at lost opportunities. The nymphs, *too conscious of their face*, were destined for the *Gnomes embrace* [I 79–80], although what this fate entails is left vague in Ariel's soothing opening speech. The Cave of Spleen will paint a grimmer picture. If the words *rage, resentment, and despair* [9] suggest that a frustrated spinsterhood and hysteric old age are

punishments for missed opportunities how does this accord with the concern for Belinda's chastity which the sylphs, the symbolism and the narrative appear to stress?

8 *Cynthia* a common name for a nymph in contemporary romantic verse, both lyric and satiric. It derives from the Roman name for the Goddess of the moon, viewed as sympathetic to lovers. **Manteau ...** a loose upper garment worn by women, a type of coat swept back to reveal the petticoat beneath. (See illustration on p. 117.)

9 Glancing back to lines 3–7 one can see that each couplet in turn gives two instances of the hostile emotions listed here, the first an epic example, the second a contemporary one either elevated or diminished by the juxtaposition depending upon how the lines are read.

15 **proper** personal, i.e. the place where he belongs.

16 *Spleen* the organ called the spleen was believed to lie on the left of the body, thus *Pain* [24] stands at the Goddess' side. Medical treatises, of which there were a great number by Pope's time since the disease had a long history, stated that it created vapours which ascended to the head, affecting the sufferer with headaches and melancholy. In Elizabethan times it was known as 'melancholy' and in Pope's time, as well as 'spleen', it was called 'hysteria', 'hypochondria' or an attack of 'the vapours'. This allows Pope to pun on the word *vapour* relating it both to the disease and to the clouds which surround Umbriel [18] and the Goddess [59] and the Cave [39].

17 **pinions** wings

18 **vapour** a cloud of mist. The Cave of Spleen is wreathed in such mists. *A constant Vapour o'er the palace flies*, creating a fitting atmosphere for a diseased region which imitates the gloom of the classical underworld and the smoky depths of Milton's Hell. *Vapour* alludes also to the mists which accompany the visionary phantoms and the theatrical transformations [40–46]. You may consider the mistiness of the scene adds to the sense that here things and people are transformed and not quite what they appear to be. Think about this in relation to lines 31–38 and 71–73.

20 **dreaded East** the chill east wind was thought to provoke attacks of spleen.

24   **Megrim** migraine, a severe headache. It was recognized that sufferers tried to avoid the light.

25   **wait** wait upon, attend.

27   **Ill-nature** what is the effect of associating ill-nature with a maiden old age? You might like to think about the picture of ageing which is presented here and in lines 29–38 and how it relates to Clarissa's speech in Canto V.

29–30   **pray'rs ... lampoons** lampoons were cruel personal attacks in writing. Tillotson suggests that the prayers are in her hand because 'though damaging they are not as damaging as lampoons which are precious enough for an unpleasant person to store in the bosom'. The lines may however be metaphorical, suggesting that apparent devotion to the welfare of others is hypocritical since, in her heart, she is merciless.

31–38   **Affectation** a primary meaning of the word is 'a striving after, aiming at'. Pope personifies a feminine striving to remain sexually alluring in defiance of the passage of time. Although *diff'ring far in figure and in face* from aged *Ill-nature*, *Affectation* cannot be young. The roses of eighteen, it is implied, are due to rouge. Her *sickness* may be a pretence which allows her to receive visitors in what she vainly hopes is a seductive state of undress, but *sickly mien* rings true. A genuinely diseased air hovers over the passage.

39   **constant Vapour** see the note on line 18.

43–46   Theatrical illusions of this type were part of the contemporary stage effects, particularly in opera and pantomime. **spires ...** coils **machines ...** stage machinery allowing angels to be suspended in air.

51   **Pipkin** small earthenware vessel. **Tripod ...** a three legged stand. Homer in the *Iliad* described a set of gold tripods made by the clever God of Smiths, Vulcan, which appeared to be self-propelled.

53   **prove with child** are pregnant.

54   The passage culminates in the most sexually allusive line of all. (See Approaches pp. 89–91.)

Lines 55–88

Umbriel's request that Belinda be touched with *chagrin* follows an explanation of how irritation, or being *in a pett* affects women generally. It spoils their looks, it spoils their behaviour and, where their behaviour is beyond reproof, Umbriel deliberately creates false rumours to cause upset anyway. Whether in beauty or behaviour, the effect of chagrin is to *spoil a grace*. What qualities are being judged as graceful or graceless? Do you feel this is a male point of view or would you agree that it is a feminine fault to become ill-tempered over beauty blemishes? The phrase *to fifty from fifteen* has a light alliterative air, in keeping with the joking tone of the passage, but could the reference to women's sexually productive years suggest that the *vapours* have a serious basis in female physiology?

55 **past** passed.
56 **Spleenwort** the epic hero Aeneas carried a golden bough as a kind of passport when he descended to the Underworld. Umbriel imitates him by carrying a fern leaf of the plant spleenwort.
60 Hysteria was thought to have a positive, creative aspect which inspired poets as well as a destructive, delusionary effect.
64 **in a pett** in a fit of ill-temper.
69 **Citron-waters** alcoholic drink, a mixture of brandy and lemon rind.
71 **airy horns** traditionally horns were the sign of a man who had an adulterous wife but *airy* means that in these instances the husband's fears are false. Umbriel is responsible for rumpling petticoats and tumbling beds, deliberately creating suspicion and havoc between husband and wife.
75 **costive** constipated.
77 **chagrin** ill-temper.
78 **half the world** presumably it is the men, not the ladies, who would be upset by a sulking Belinda.
82 *Ulysses* at the end of ten-year siege of Troy, Ulysses, one of the Greek chiefs, was fated to wander the seas for a further

ten years before he could return home to his faithful wife
Penelope. On his voyages he stopped at the island belonging
to Aeolus, Warden of the Gales, who made him a present of a
leathern bag in which were imprisoned all the adverse winds.

85 **Vial** small glass bottle.

Lines 89–120

Belinda is dejected by the loss of her lock but neither aroused nor
angry until Umbriel opens the bag of discontented winds over her
head. Thalestris' speech increases her fury. Does this go any way
to excusing her behaviour in Canto V?

What picture of beauty is given by the words *durance, bound,
tort'ring, strain'd, bravely bore the double loads of lead*? These images
of Belinda being imprisoned and tortured by her beauty-aids are
similar to those Ariel threatens the sylphs with in Canto II
123–136. There the tone was humorous; here you may sense a
more serious air. Of the two pictures we are given of Belinda's
toilette, in Canto II and Canto IV, which do you find the more
realistic, which the more truthful? (And are these necessarily the
same?) The point of the self-inflicted punishment is raised but the
question, *Was it for this* …? is left for the reader to answer.

Thalestris makes much of the *unrival'd shrine* of Honour at
which, she claims, *all* is resigned. What sort of honour can be lost
in a whisper? Is Thalestris using the word in the same sense as the
sylphs in Canto II when they set out to guard Belinda equally
against a stain on *her honour* or her *new brocade* [II 107]? Like the
sylphs, she appears to equate appearance, the reputation for
virtue, with the real thing, but does Pope and should Belinda?

89 ***Thalestris*** Queen of the Amazons, in Greek mythology a
race of warrior women.

92 **vent** opening.

99–101 These lines paint a picture of the trouble it took to create
ringlets and locks with curling papers. *Fillets* were head-bands
sometimes made of metal.

106   Is *all* meaningless or a revealing slip of the tongue?

114   **Expos'd thro' crystal** the Baron plans to wear the lock in a crystal ring, set with diamonds, which will allow the hair to show through the clear glass.

117   *Hyde-park Circus* the fashionable drive in Hyde Park. (See also the note on line I 44.)

118   *Bow* St Mary le Bow was the traditional centre of the mercantile City of London. Being born within the sound of Bow bells identified one as a local, as opposed to the more fashionable West End where wits would expect to live.

Lines 121–140

The Baron's firm defence contrasts with the hesitant approach of Sir Plume. Consider their different speech patterns. Sir Plume's has broken, incomplete phrasing, ejaculations and oaths. His request, when he finally manages to get it out, is blunt to the point of rudeness. One feels that the Baron's elegant and ironic reproof, enjoyed by the reader, passes over his head. The Baron's reply is expressed in a single, lengthy, balanced sentence. Do you feel this is same effete hero we met in Canto II, sacrificing at Love's altar, or does he gain in stature by this exchange?

124   **nice conduct** neat flourish. **Clouded cane** … streaked or mottled walking stick.

137   The Baron's grand claim will be ironically fulfilled in Canto V when his *vital air* is blocked by a sneeze caused by the snuff Belinda throws at him and he indeed loses the lock.

Lines 141–176

Pope models Belinda's lament on a famous passage in the *Iliad* where Achilles mourns his fallen friend Patroclus. Pope's tone is that of a young coquette complaining, (e.g. *and* Shock *was most unkind!*) Where he borrows language from the epic (e.g. *For ever curs'd be this detested day*) Belinda's distress seems humorously exaggerated. At other points the exaggeration creates a sense of innocence. Is it likely she would rather have remain'd *un-admir'd* especially in *some lone isle*? She seems very young in these lines. Not to know *what mov'd her mind with youthful Lords to roam* is to retreat to childhood. And if we feel that she could, on reflection, answer her own question would she have spoken the final couplet if she had realized the sexual *double-entendre* it contained?

156   **Bohea** an expensive variety of tea.
162   **patch-box** the patches worn by women as fashionable beauty marks were kept in ornamented boxes.
164   **Poll** Belinda's parrot.
175–176   The reader is expected to recognize that Belinda is offering to sacrifice the essence of her virtue for its outward appearance. The question is whether she herself realizes the implications of her words. Are they spoken knowingly, echoing Thalestris' claim in line 106, or do they establish her essential innocence and youth?

Canto V

Lines 1–34

Clarissa claims that her advice to Belinda (to strive to be *first in virtue* as she is in *face*) is common sense. With the loss of beauty comes the loss of power over the opposite sex. It is *good sense* therefore to *preserve what beauty gains* by *charms* which are more lasting. In her generous plea for *good-humour still, whate'er we lose*, Clarissa can be seen as the heroine of the poem, the only character who successfully translates the epic concept of honour to the contemporary scene without losing all sense of virtue.

Alternatively, she can be seen as the voice of experience, teaching Belinda with a knowing air how to hold on to a man. Do you find her advice moral or practical? Is she wise or is she worldly-wise? The unanswered questions pile up [9–14] and it is worth trying to answer them, for your answers will help you to decide for yourself something about which critics disagree: what is meant by Clarissa's final warning, *well our pow'r to use*.

Eighteenth-century readers would have recognized that Clarissa's speech was modelled on Sarpedon's call-to-arms in the *Iliad*. Pope had translated and published this famous episode before commencing his full translation of the *Iliad*. See Appendix 3 for Pope's translation of the speech. In his speech the epic hero Sarpedon inspires his companion Glaucus by comparing an honourable and valiant death in battle with an ignoble old age. Although we are expected to see a mocking contrast between courage in the face of death and good humour in the face of decay, you may feel that some of the grandeur of the original passage is caught in the tone of these lines.

Pope did not add Clarissa's speech to *The Rape* until he published the third version in 1717. He claimed that he did so 'to open more clearly the MORAL of the Poem'. Some readers see Clarissa as the moral centre of the poem, but not all do. Others argue that the conclusion proves that Belinda wins more by passion and pride than she would ever have achieved by remaining placidly good-humoured. And many regard the poem as a joke which requires no moral. There remains critical disagreement about Clarissa's speech. Does it encapsulate, change or avoid the moral of the poem? Or is the *Rape* an affectionate and teasing picture of a day in the life of a belle which we misread if we search seriously for a moral?

2 *Jove* the Roman name for the King of the Gods, also known as Jupiter or, in Greek mythology, as Zeus.

5–6 **the *Trojan*** is Aeneas who, urged by the Gods, abandoned his lover *Dido*, Queen of Carthage, and continued on to Italy to fulfill his destiny of founding Rome. When Dido saw Aeneas' men preparing a fleet of ships and guessed that he was about to leave her, she broke out in furious accusations. Her speeches failed to alter his resolve so she sent her sister Anna to him with tearful but equally fruitless messages.

14 **side-box** box at the side of a theatre.

17 **front-box** the front-boxes in a theatre were nearest to the stage and set at an angle which gave the audience a clear view of whoever sat in them.

20 **small-pox** a highly contagious and often fatal disease until Jenner's discovery in 1796 of the cowpox vaccine. If victims survived the attack they were left disfigured, their faces pitted with pock marks. In the Eighteenth century it was sufficient to have a clear complexion to be considered a beauty. The poem's obsession with cosmetics glosses over a reality which surfaces here, reverberating with warnings in spite of the light tone. Is it, after all, *a sin to paint*?

A particular pang may have been felt by those intimate with the Petres and Fermors because Lord Petre died of the smallpox in 1713, two years after the first version of the poem and four years before Pope added Clarissa's speech.

23 **patch** (see the note on line I 138) **ogle**... glance flirtatiously.

Lines 35–102

The sexual nature of the encounter between Belinda and the Baron is made clear in the *double-entendres* in these lines, some blatant [78, 98, 102], some more ambiguous [44, 67–70]. Belinda appears still to regard the contest as a struggle for the lock, but the Baron is well aware of what he has lost by his earlier attack. Not he but *some other* will win the lady. The joke of applying an epic lineage to the bodkin and the heroic tone of 45–52 do not entirely ridicule the Baron. What commenced as trophy-hunting has turned into a true passion. There is a real sense of loss in his speech *Boast not my fall* [97–100] from a man who claims he *sought no more*, in whichever sense we choose to read that ambiguous phrase. Do you find your attitude softening towards the Baron as he reveals himself as susceptible and vulnerable? Has he become victim rather than aggressor? Or are we being invited to view both him and Belinda as victim and aggressor at the same time?

35 **no applause ensu'd** if Clarissa's plea to value good humour and good sense above charm and beauty is indeed the moral (See the general note on lines 1–34) then, within the poem, it falls on deaf ears. And any certainty that Pope intends such a moral to be taken, if not by Belinda at least by the reader, is belied by what happens finally to the lock and to her name in lines 149–150.

37 **Virago** a female warrior.

40 **whalebones** were used to stiffen women's clothing, particularly undergarments, such as corsets and girdles.

42 **base** bass.

44 **mortal** is the wound mortal because it is fatal or because it is inflicted and sustained by men as opposed to Gods? The first meaning mocks the bravery of *Heroes* who battle against *fans* and *whalebones*: the second has sexual implications, the wounds of human passion.

47 ***Pallas*** ... Pallas Athene, Goddess of Wisdom; ***Mars*** ... God of War; ***Latona*** ... Goddess mother of Apollo and Diana; ***Hermes*** ... messenger of the Gods.

48 ***Olympus*** Mount Olympus in Greece was believed to be the home of the Gods.

50 ***Neptune*** God of the Sea.

53 **sconce** wall-bracket to hold candles, often backed with a mirror to increase the light by reflection.

55 **bodkin** these useful instruments, either needles or decorative pins (see lines 88–96) are here transformed into spears emphasizing the diminutive nature of the sylphs and also their intrinsically domestic concerns.

59 **Witling** a fop possessed of little wit.

60–66 The beaux (no longer referred to as heroes, but given the names of foppish characters, such as *Dapperwit* and Sir *Fopling Flutter*, from Restoration Comedies) 'die' with phrases from theatre and opera on their lips. The romantic clichés contrast with the epic language of lines 45–52 and the seriousness with which the fops take themselves is mocked by the descent from grand, heroic phraseology. The sexual meaning of the verb 'to die' (for males, to achieve a climax and lose arousal) suggests that the sexual battle is real. Is there also a literary joke; an implication that the wits' metaphors and songs are full of borrowed, hackneyed phrases and second-hand language because their wooing is insincere and unoriginal?

65 **Mæander** the name of the river echoes the verb 'to meander' or wander slowly.

66 **Swan** refers to the poetic legend that swans sing once only, at the moment of death.

68 **Chloe** a common name for belles in light poetry.

69–70 Note how Sir Plume goes down a *hero* but rises again as a *Beau*. Is this another example of the mocking juxtaposition of epic and colloquial styles or is there a sexual connotation in the revival of a lover?

73–74 **beam** the crosspiece of the scales from which are suspended two pans in which the wits and the hair are weighed against each other. Do you think the barely perceptible difference in weight compliments Belinda or equates her lock with the wits which have been discredited in the previous lines?

77–78 If the fight were primarily a show of physical strength *unequal* would be a strange adjective since the sense clearly indicates that it is Belinda who is the stronger opponent. All is explained by the second line of the couplet where the Baron's desire to make love to Belinda is clear. In the sense of 'only', *no more* shows the inherent weakness of his position. His will waits upon her agreement. Is there another meaning to *no more*, an ironic sense that *more* than this he could not hope for?

82 **Snuff** tobacco in a finely powdered form which was sniffed up the nostrils. The pinch of snuff which Belinda throws at the Baron causes a sneeze that completely subdues him.

88 **deadly** after stressing the minuteness of the bodkins used by the sylphs as spears can Pope intend this word seriously?

Lines 103–150

Images and themes which run through the poem come to their culmination in the concluding lines: the sun image, the transformations, the allusions to myths and legends about people translated at death into heavenly bodies. Do you feel a sense of melancholy in these lines; an admission that underlying the exaggerated claims for Belinda's beauty there always lay an awareness of its transience? Is this balanced by the promise that her lock and her name will survive? Or does the reappearance of the Muse show us that Pope believes the true source of glory is neither Belinda's beauty nor her lock, but his poetry?

91 **seal-rings** rings with engraved stamps on their faces which were used to impress a pattern on sealing wax to seal a letter or validate a legal document.

105 *Othello* in Shakespeare's play of the same name, the hero Othello is driven distracted by jealousy of his innocent wife Desdemona. A crucial element in the false accusations brought against her by his evil lieutenant, Iago, is a precious handkerchief which Othello gave her as a love gift. There are several speeches in the play which express his distress including one where he falls into an epileptic fit.

109 **guilt ... pain** *force* or *fraud* [II 32], *force or slight* [II 103], *stratagems* [III 120] and *mischief* [III 125] have all been associated with the Baron's rape of the lock. This is the first suggestion of guilt or pain.

113 **Lunar sphere** the airy region which lay between earth and moon (and below the eternal sphere) was under the influence of the moon. It was inhabited by the sylphs [II 81] and filled, if we are to believe the description of the following lines, with the discarded trivia of the Beau-monde, along with items which hint at the falsity of human emotion and the waste of human endeavour.

117 **alms** gifts or money for the poor. The implication in *death-bed alms* is that miserly people give only under the fear of damnation.

122 **tomes of casuistry** unreadably long books of dull, scholarly argument.

125–126 Romulus, the legendary founder of Rome, was translated to the heavens at his death, appearing in a vision to Proculus.

129 *Berenice's* **Locks** a figure in classical legend whose locks were similarly turned into stars.

133 ***Beau-monde*** the social world of beaux and belles. **Mall** a tree-lined avenue beside the royal palace of St James, a very fashionable place for walking, driving or playing Pall-mall, a kind of croquet.

135 ***Venus*** Goddess of Love.

136 ***Rosamonda's* lake** Rosamond's pond in St James Park was a notorious meeting place for lovers.

137 ***Partridge*** published almanacks annually in Pope's time making ridiculous predictions which never failed to include the downfall of the Pope (*the fall of Rome*) and the King of France (*the fate of Louis*).

138 ***Galilæo's* eyes** Galileo was an Italian astronomer of the late Sixteenth and early Seventeenth centuries, who was an early inventor of telescopes.

139 **egregious** absurd.

Approaches

Pope's life

At the time of Pope's birth his father was a linen merchant in London. Both his parents were Roman Catholics and Pope continued in the faith all his life, although to do so meant that he had to accept the legal restrictions and civil disadvantages which were increasingly imposed upon Roman Catholics after the exile of James II in 1688 and the reaffirming of Protestant rule under William and Mary. He could not attend university, he could not hold public office or practise a profession, he could not live within ten miles of London. The threat of financial penalties hung over him as it did over all of his faith. With firmness and a certain nonchalance he parried his friend Bishop Atterbury's plea to change his religion, 'that Accident to your Own Ease and Happiness', by claiming that he lacked ambition, suffered from poor health and that it would upset his mother. These excuses may have hidden a faith deeper than he cared to reveal to his Protestant friends.

The laws against Catholics residing within ten miles of the capital probably account for the family's removal when Pope was twelve years old to a place which was bliss for the boy, the village of Binfield in Windsor Forest. Pope loved the Forest and made the first of his valuable friendships there, with Sir William Trumbull, a former Secretary of State, with John Caryll, the instigator of *The Rape of the Lock*, and with the Blount sisters at Mapledurham House to whom he would later write some of his most loving poems. But when he was about thirteen he caught a disease which seems to have been a form of spinal tuberculosis. It left him physically deformed. He never grew above four and a half feet high. His body became twisted and hunchbacked and the effort of standing and moving showed in cords of tension which stood out in his face in later life. Inhibited by his appearance, although always ready to joke about it, he never married.

In his late teens he made his way back to London in the hope of publishing his earliest poems. There he met the ageing poet and playwright William Wycherley, and through him and through the convenient meeting place of recently fashionable coffee houses, he got to know London's leading literary men. Some, like Swift and Gay, became life-long friends. In 1709 his first poems were published and included among them was his translation of the episode of Sarpedon from the *Iliad*, a translation he was to parody in *The Rape of the Lock*. For a while he kept up an active social life in London, but after his father's death in 1717 he rented a house in Twickenham, close to his London friends and a safe enough distance away to qualify under the ten mile rule. Here, in semi-retirement with his mother, gardening and writing poetry, he lived modestly on the income from his father's estate and the considerable profits from his translations of the *Iliad* and the *Odyssey* between 1713 and 1725. From each of these publishing ventures he made between four and five thousand pounds, while for *The Rape of the Lock*, although it was a bestseller, he received only fifteen pounds.

Pope was disadvantaged in public life as he was disabled in private. Poetry and friendship took the place of business and marriage, his genius for both heightened perhaps by the restrictions he suffered. *The Muse but serv'd ... to help me thro' this long Disease, my Life*, he wrote towards the end of his life in a poem addressed to his friend and physician, Dr Arbuthnot.

> Friend to my life (which did not you prolong
> The World had wanted many an idle Song).

It is typical of Pope that he composed the poem quickly as a gift and testament, having learned that Dr Arbuthnot was dying. The first version of *The Rape of the Lock*, the greatest of his early poems, was also written at speed and as an act of friendship.

The occasion of the poem

The occasion of the poem was a quarrel between two land-owning Roman Catholic families, the Petres and the Fermors. We know only the barest details of the incident. Lord Petre cut

off a lock of Miss Arabella Fermor's hair. As Pope explained to
his friend Spence:

> The stealing of Miss Belle Fermor's hair was taken too
> seriously, and caused an estrangement between the two
> families, though they had lived so long in great friendship
> before. A common acquaintance and well-wisher to both,
> desired me to write a poem to make a jest of it, and laugh
> them together again. It was with this view that I wrote the
> *Rape of the Lock.*

Belle Fermor was a society beauty whose good looks had been
celebrated in verse by several poets. Lord Petre had succeeded to
his Essex estate in his teens, under the guardianship of John
Caryll who was a close friend of Pope. Pope himself barely knew
Arabella, if at all, and he never met Lord Petre. It was John
Caryll, the *common acquaintance*, who was the real instigator of
the poem.

   The age of the principals, both in their early twenties, suggests
a romantic escapade, but if this was so the courtship was abortive.
Before the poem was published Lord Petre was married, and not
to Arabella, who wed a Berkshire gentleman a few years later.

Versions

The Rape exists in three distinct versions. In answer to Caryll's
request, Pope wrote his first two-canto poem quickly in 1711. He
circulated it privately to the parties concerned and published it
(whether with or without their permission remains unclear) in
1712. This version of the poem forms Appendix 2 on pp. 122–
131. In 1714 he enlarged his two cantos to five, introducing *the
Machinery*, that band of aerial beings who accompany and
attempt to protect Belinda, and adding to the number of mock-
epic incidents.

   Pope's third version was for his collected *Works* in 1717 when
he added Clarissa's speech in Canto V. With some minor

alterations taken from his 1736 edition of his *Works* this is the text which has been used for this edition.

Epic and mock-epic

Pope called *The Rape, an heroi-comical poem*, by which he meant a mock-epic. He could assume that his eighteenth-century readers, educated in the classics and knowledgeable about epics, would recognize that it was a mockery. Many of his jokes rest upon this assumption. For the modern reader notes identifying the sources of his parodies are helpful, but a better way of appreciating how the humour of his exaggerated style derives from the epic is to read, even in part, translations of the classical Greek epic, the *Iliad* by Homer; or the Roman epic, the *Aeneid* by Virgil; or the English epic, *Paradise Lost* by John Milton.

Epic subjects were grand: the Trojan wars, the founding of Rome, the fall of Man; and were narrated at length in twelve or more books, each consisting of several hundred lines. The epic hero traversed a wide geographical area over a long period of time, encountering battles, romantic interludes, journeys by land and sea, even a descent into the underworld. From on high the gods watched the human drama, intervening when they chose at critical moments. Success for the hero was dependent upon the subplot of divine intrigue as well as his own courage and skill. His fate was ordained. Honour, the epic ideal, lay in journeying on, fighting bravely and accepting whatever end the gods had willed.

The form and style of an epic was so clearly recognized by Pope's time that he teasingly drew up a set of rules for aspiring epic poets *without a Genius, nay without Learning or much Reading. This must necessarily be of great Use to all those Poets who confess they never Read, and of whom the World is convinced they never learn.* He published the following spoof (*The Guardian* 10 June 1713) in the manner of a cooking recipe.

A Receipt to make an Epick Poem
    Take out of any old Poem, History-books, Romance, or
    Legend . . . those parts of Story which afford most Scope for

> long Descriptions: Put these Pieces together, and throw all
> the Adventures you fancy into one Tale. Then take a Hero,
> whom you may chuse for the Sound of his Name, and put him
> into the midst of these Adventures: There let him work, for
> twelve Books . . .

He continues in the same mocking manner, laying down rules for
writing descriptions,

> Pick a large quantity of Images and Descriptions from Homer's
> Iliad, with a Spice or two of Virgil,

and choosing language,

> Here it will do well to be an Imitator of Milton, for you'll find it
> easier to imitate him in this than any thing else.

The mock-epic, also an established literary form in Pope's time,
imitated the most recognizable aspects of the epic, its form and
elevated language. It used an inflated style to ridicule the
pretentions and pomposity of minor quarrels. It exposed the
limitations of contemporary society by the implicit contrast with
an expansive epic world. The idle pursuits of the beau monde and
the low pursuits of the inner city were shown to be unworthy of a
literary form firmly associated with heroes.

At the same time as he was writing *The Rape*, Pope was also
engaged in translating Homer's *Iliad*. Translations of epics were
highly regarded and better paid than original poetry. Pope was
financially so successful in this venture that he went on to
translate Homer's *Odyssey*, albeit with the help of unacknow-
ledged contributors. He read widely in earlier English translations
of Virgil and Homer and from these he borrowed elaborate
phrases for the *Rape*. He borrowed from *Paradise Lost*. Again and
again Pope's language would not be out of place in a serious epic.
The joke lies in his applying this elevated language to *the life of
modern ladies in this idle town* as he deprecatingly described the
subject of *The Rape* in a letter to a lady friend.

The opening

Homer set the pattern for epic openings in the *Iliad*. This is Pope's translation of the opening lines.

> Achilles' Wrath, to Greece the direful Spring
> Of Woes unnumber'd, heav'nly Goddess, sing!

The subject of the poem is announced immediately. This is called the 'proposition'. The poet then calls upon a Goddess or Muse to inspire his song. This is the 'invocation'. For added emphasis normal syntax (the word order of the sentence) is reversed. Object precedes verb, and the object of the verb is the subject of the epic.

Activity

In a similar style Virgil commences the *Aeneid*. Here is Dryden's translation which Pope knew well. See if you can identify the proposition, the subject of the poem, and discover who it is the poet calls upon for inspiration.

> Arms, and the man I sing, who forc'd by fate,
> And haughty Juno's unrelenting hate,
> Expell'd and exil'd, left the *Trojan* shore;
> Long labours, both by Sea and Land he bore
> And in the doubtful War, before he won
> The Latian Realm, and built the destin'd Town;
> His banish'd Gods restored to Rites Divine,
> And setl'd sure Succession in his Line:
> From whence the Race of Albian Fathers come,
> 10   And the long glories of Majestic Rome.
>   Oh Muse! the Causes and the Crimes relate,
> What goddess was provok'd, and whence her hate:
> For what Offence the queen of Heav'n began
> To persecute so brave, so just a Man!

The proposition of the epic is *Arms, and the man.* The opening paragraph describes his deeds and from these clues a contemporary reader would recognize him as Aeneas who, driven from Troy, founded the *destin'd Town* of Rome. The poet calls on the *Muse* to *relate* the story, as though he could not do it without her aid.

The subject of the poem, *Arms, and the man*, is placed before the verb *sing*, of which it is the grammatical object. This is a reversal of the normal word order of the English sentence; subject, verb, object. In the same way Milton turns the long opening sentence of *Paradise Lost*, with an even greater distance between the main verb and its object. Can you identify the subject of the poem and the main verb of the sentence?

> Of man's first disobedience, and the fruit
> Of that forbidden tree, whose mortal taste
> Brought death into the world, and all our woe,
> With loss of Eden, till one greater man
> Restore us, and regain the blissful seat,
> Sing, heavenly Muse, that on the secret top
> Of Oreb, or of Sinai, didst inspire
> That shepherd, who first taught the chosen seed
> In the beginning how the heavens and earth
> 10 Rose out of chaos: or, if Sion hill
> Delight thee more, and Siloa's brook that flowed
> Fast by the oracle of God; I thence
> Invoke thy aid to my adventu'rous song
> That with no middle flight intends to soar
> Above the Aonian mount, while it pursues
> Things unattempted yet in prose or rhyme,
> And chiefly thou O Spirit, that dost prefer
> Before all temples the upright heart and pure,
> Instruct me, for thou know'st; thou from the first
> 20 Wast present, and with mighty wings outspread
> Dove-like sat'st brooding on the vast abyss
> And madest it pregnant: what in me is dark
> Illumine, what is low raise and support;
> That to the highth of this great argument
> I may assert eternal providence,
> And justify the ways of God to men.

Milton's syntax follows the pattern of the opening of an epic. He announces his poem's subject in the first line (*man's first disobedience and the fruit of that forbidden tree*) but the main verb *Sing* is delayed until line 6. The remainder of his long sentence is given over to subordinate clauses describing the Christianized Muse whose aid he invokes [13] and [22–23] and who is the subject of his main verb.

Pope consciously imitates the epic opening in his first twelve lines. He too will *sing* [3] his subject whose importance he indicates by inverted syntax and elevated language: *dire offence, mighty contests, tasks so bold*. He invokes inspiration. He addresses the Muse. His tone has the declamatory epic ring as he commands the Goddess, *Say what strange motive* [7].

At some point, and not too far into the poem, readers should sense that Pope is mocking the epic form and laughing at his subject. Try reading the first three paragraphs again [1–26]. Can you find a moment when you felt the poem might be a joke? For me it is the idea of the sleepless lovers who do not wake until noon.

Once we realize that we are reading a mock-epic it casts a different light on the apparent solemnity and dignity of Pope's proposition and invocation.

Activity

Read Canto I 1–12. Do these lines depart in any way from the conventional epic opening? Can you identify any hint of mockery in the lines?

Discussion

It seems that the first hint of the mock-epic comes in line 3 where Pope credits a human rather than the Muse with inspiring his poem. The ambiguity of *ev'n Belinda* has been mentioned (See note I 4). With lines 5–6 we can be more certain. Epic causes may be amorous or trivial; epic subjects are never slight. From then on Pope's irony becomes clearer. Words appropriate to different and conflicting spheres of action appear together; *well-bred lord* and *gentle Belle* belong in the elegant drawing room; *assault* on the battlefield (or in the back-alley?). Their inappropriate juxtaposition suggests mockery while leaving open the question of what is mocked. The implications of lines 9–10 are that the Belle is self-interested, not heroic. And can we take Pope seriously when he asks in the elevated language of the epic whether *tasks so bold*, are fit for *little men*?

Finally there is the matter of tone. Pope's opening has an easy tone in contrast to Milton's weighty words and learned references. Perhaps the clearest distinction between epic and mock-epic is the contrast in the attitude of each poet to his task; Milton's humility, *what in me is dark Illumine, what is low raise* and Pope's elated claim, *Slight is the subject but not so the praise.*

The setting

A glittering world of wealth

The setting of the poem shimmers with wealth. It depicts a world of luxurious things: silks, watches, gems, cases, snuff-boxes, fans, caskets, canes, screens, mirrors, vases, chinaware. The lives of Belinda and the Baron are cossetted by rich objects and the adjectives associated with them add to their lustre: *gilded, silver, sparkling, speckled, gilt, shining, rich, painted, glitt'ring.*

What should we feel about this accumulation of wealthy possessions? The atmosphere created by the adjectives might suggest that Pope delights in the exquisite craftsmanship and beauty of precious objects. In phrases such as *gratify their scent and taste* [III 111] and *beauty draws us with a single hair* [II 28] he appears to share his character's enjoyment of fine things. Other phrases however are more critical of their pampered lives.

The instructive hours spent at court are passed in *various talk* [III 11] which Pope refers to a few lines later as *chat.* What sort of learning is summed up in the word 'chat'? And what are the implications of the closing phrase of the couplet:

> Snuff, or the fan, supply each pause of chat,
> With singing, laughing, ogling, and all that.   [III 17–18]

The dismissive tone of *and all that* implies that Pope is judging the *instructive hours* and finding them wanting, in both educational and moral terms. Similarly there are moments when Pope appears to mock his characters' possessions and it is difficult to know whether his attitude is indulgently teasing or highly critical. For example, consider the Baron's altar to love built from *twelve vast French Romances, neatly gilt*. How seriously can we treat this and his sacrifice of *three garters, half a pair of gloves*?

What are the connotations of *vast* in the line describing the French Romances? The adjective may refer to the physical size of the books (but should romances be so weighty?) or their length (are these books unreadably long?). *Vast* could mean intolerable or magnificent. The tone seems to be simultaneously hostile and admiring. And what of *gilt*? The word appears to stress the books' value and attractiveness but equally the neatness of the gilt might suggest that they have never been opened, let alone read.

Activity

What is the tone of the following couplets? Do you detect mockery or approval?

> This casket *India's* glowing gems unlocks,
> And all *Arabia* breathes from yonder box.   [I 133–134]

> But now secure the painted vessel glides,
> The sun-beams trembling on the floating tydes: [II 47–48]

> For lo! the board with cups and spoons is crown'd,
> The berries crackle, and the mill turns round;   [III 105–106]

Discussion

Do you feel that Pope delights in the sensuousness of the objects he describes? If the last quotation on page 78 is read aloud, it sounds almost Dickensian in its enjoyment of grinding coffee beans.

In brief, Pope's descriptions of luxurious things create a gilded setting for his poem. If the tone hints at times a critical attitude towards those who enjoy the luxury, at other times he seems to have fallen under the spell of the precious things he describes. Many of the poem's phrases show Pope balancing delicately between disapproval and teasing.

Bright Inhabitants of the Air

Precious possessions are not the only things which glitter in the poem. There are also the irridescent, shimmering sylphs.

Activity

Read Canto II 59–70. Does the language suggest a connection between the sylphs and the material objects in the poem?

Some of the words in this passage (*gold, glitt'ring, richest, gilded*) are adjectives which Pope used of the wealthy setting. Their presence here suggests that the sylphs too are part of the poem's glittering ambience, reflecting and contributing to the radiant atmosphere. Other words stress their *half-dissolv'd, filmy, transparent* forms and their restless movement; *waft, 'fluid, loose, disports, colours that change.* If you concentrate upon these words the sylphs appear thin and insubstantial beside the solidity of chariots and barges, snuff-boxes and coffee pots. They share the colours of the earthly world but lack its substance; e.g. the shears which sever Belinda's locks have no effect on the sylphs because *airy substance soon unites again,* [III 152]

The thinness of their glitter is even clearer if you compare them with the human protagonists. They lack warmth. They are unmoved by the desires which inflame Belinda and the Baron and at the climax, they are powerless in the face of passions they do not possess. Their fluid, transparent qualities may be a hint that their powers will fade away when confronted by the reality of warm human feelings.

Beauty and fragility

A significant number of things in Belinda's world are expensive and beautiful but also delicate, fragile and easily broken. Three times in the poem the fragility of china is mentioned.

> Or when rich *China* vessels, fall'n from high,
> In glitt'ring dust, and painted fragments lie!   [III 159–160]

> Or some frail *China* jar receive a flaw   [II 106]

> The tott'ring China shook without a wind   [IV 163]

Like the cracking of delicate chinaware, brocade can be stained, necklaces lost, petticoats fail and a lock of hair vanish. Everything precious is vulnerable. Perhaps this is an essential part of preciousness. What does this suggest about the most beautiful thing in the poem, Belinda herself?

When her toilette is completed and her beauty is at its most flawless, Belinda issues forth to rival the sun. With all the hints about the vulnerability and fragility of precious objects, are you surprised to find that in spite of all her efforts, all Betty's efforts and all the sylphs' efforts, *frail beauty must decay?* [V 25] Clarissa spells out the fate which beautiful girls share with precious possessions: *painted, or not painted, all shall fade.* [V 27] Nothing saves them from the ravages of time.

Activity

Read Canto II 105–110. Compare what happens to objects and what happens to young girls.

Discussion

The incongruity of the pairings gives a ridiculous air to the lines, creating a joking tone which suggests that the events are all accidental and should not be taken seriously. Perhaps it strains against the laughing mood of the passage to point out the obvious, that, for most people, the loss of virginity and the chipping of china are events of incomparably different orders of seriousness. The passage can be read as teasing mockery which has no intention of making reasonable sense. It could be a comment (affectionate or ironic or critical) on a world of style where values belong to appearances and where good taste and polite behaviour are as important as honour and chastity.

The juxtaposition of material accidents and moral failings could imply a connection as well as an ironic contrast between china and chastity. Cracked vases, stained brocades and lost necklaces are images of Belinda's chastity which, the critic Cleanth Brooks has written, is like fine porcelain, *brittle, precious, useless and easily broken*. You may argue that, far from being useless, Belinda's innocence is part of her seductive appeal for the Baron but is it ridiculous to equate a young girl's virginity with objects of rare and delicate fragility?

The mercantile background

So far we have considered objects as though they operated in the poem as part of the background to Belinda's world or as images. But these objects were also real artifacts in the lives of a wealthy section of eighteenth-century society. Take, for instance, the three familiar beverages consumed in the poem; tea, chocolate and coffee. These entered England in the Mid-Seventeenth century as an experimental addition to the East India Company's cargoes of silks and spices. Coffee houses started up in London in the late Seventeenth century and by the time of *The Rape* they had become fashionable rendez-vous for businessmen. Tea trickled in more slowly. Sales expanded significantly only at the beginning of the Eighteenth century when its high import duty was reduced. Pepys mentions in his diary drinking his first *Cupp of Tee* in 1660 and the drink was so new that it was spelt variously as tee, tay and tea, tcha, cha and chaw. Coffee drinking was normally a public occasion; tea was considered a ladies' drink and served privately, although Queen Anne offered it as evening entertainment at Hampton Court.

Activity

Read Canto III 107–118. What might have been the attitude of contemporary readers to the things Pope describes?

Discussion

When infusing coffee is exaggerated into raising *fiery spirits* on *Altars of Japan* and cups turn into *China's earth*, you may well decide the tone is pompous and mocking. But the status of tea and coffee drinking at that period could account for the description seeming almost reverential. Eighteenth-century readers would recognize the silver lamp, Japanese lacquer and China porcelain as expensive, exotic, imported commodities. Most of the objects in the poem are modish, stylish, costly items of conspicuous consumption. This throws a somewhat different light on the sylphs, trembling lest Belinda spill coffee on her brocade.

These luxury items bear witness to England's rising prosperity and mercantile expansion. They are the benefits of her trading success with the then-known world. Belinda is adorned with *Unnumber'd treasures* and *various off'rings of the world* [I 129–130]. The labour which created, the merchants who transported, and the wealth which paid for the things which deck her are not mentioned directly yet it may be that Pope is not altogether mocking when, a few lines later, he calls her beauty *awful*.

At the toilette Betty arrays Belinda in glittering *spoil*. What does the word convey to you? One of its primary meanings is the loot which marauding armies seize. To make off with whatever he could carry was a victorious soldier's right. In this sense Belinda's lock can be seen as battle-spoil; as the gain which the conquering Baron will seize upon. The aggressive and military language used for his designs (*By force to ravish, or by fraud betray* [II 32]) suggests a chieftain plotting a campaign.

Thalestris refers to the lock [IV 113] as *th'inestimable prize*. The lock can be read as a metaphor for the lady herself and the decking of Belinda in *spoil* may suggest that she herself is the prize.

If however we treat the lock as spoil in the mercantile sense it implies an article chosen carefully with an eye to its economic value. Belinda rises from her toilette a finished product, an object of desire. Luxury objects are desirable because they confer status on the possessor. Has Belinda become a 'thing' to be owned and displayed? Is she prized because she is beautiful, expensive, precious and, once possessed by man, a sign of his conspicuous consumption?

The sylphs

The sylphs are Pope's mocking re-creation of the gods who watch over the heroes of epics and guide their fortunes. It is nicely fitting that Pope's supernatural beings, who are supposed to imitate Homer's deities and Milton's angels, are tiny, frail and powerless. Far from taking a decisive part in the action these flimsy creatures are afraid of human men. *An earthly Lover lurking at her heart* [III 144] is all it takes to frighten them away. Although they are an amalgam of epic machinery, Rosicrucian lore (See the notes on I 13–120) and English folk tale, they are essentially Pope's invention. As Dr Johnson pointed out, we need no background information to picture them.

> A race of aerial people, never heard of before, is presented to us in a manner so clear and easy, that the reader seeks for no more information.

Activity

How would you describe, or draw, a sylph? Which phrase or phrases best capture the essentials of their appearance?

Discussion

I see them as small, winged creatures, like iridescent dragonflies. They are *ever on the wing* [I 43]; they *flutter* [I 66] on *insect wing,* [II 59] and their fluid forms are *transparent* [II 61] to the reader (*tho' unseen* [I 43] by humans in the poem). *Thin glitt'ring textures of the filmy dew* [II 64] or *half-dissolv'd in light* [II 62] are key phrases for me. How tiny they are! They even seem to diminish in size as the narrative continues. Ariel hovering over Belinda's head in Canto I was a favourite scene with the poem's illustrators. In the Eighteenth century they tended to depict him as a winged Cupid, in the Nineteenth as a fairy doll, but always of sufficient size to be clearly visible. Yet in Canto II fifty sylphs are required to surround Belinda's petticoat and in Canto III one thousand close in to protect her lock.

Their duties are solely concerned with female adornment and female behaviour, both of which are portrayed as elegant and graceful like the sylphs. There is no equivalent machinery to guard or guide the men in the poem. Why do the women alone require protection and what are we to make of this indication of their fragility and weakness? Is Belinda's status enhanced by the presence of a troop of celestial beings whose entire *raison d'etre* is to perfect and protect her appearance, or do the sylphs suggest a trivialising and enfeebling concern with her own attractions?

The sylphs of course take their duties seriously. Is the joke against them for attempting to assume the epic role in a society devoted to pleasure or can they justify the moral tone of their language? They use the high epic term *Honour* [I 78] as though it were synonymous with themselves.

Activity

Read Canto I 67–104. What do you think Ariel means by the word honour?

Discussion

The word honour is elusive and undefined in the poem. Honour—or sylph—(syntactically the words are interchangeable) *guards the purity* of maids. To equate it baldly with virginity loses the seductive charm of the passage. These Maids [71] are *melting* with *warm desires*. They court sexual encounters at balls and masquerades and the sylphs' protection does not inhibit such encounters but encourages and increases them. The sylphs claim to be on the side of virginity; *whoever fair and chaste Rejects mankind, is by some Sylph embrac'd* [I 67–68] but women who refuse proposals and deny love are predestined for the Gnomes' embrace. Where do the sylphs stand?

Thalestris uses the word *Honour* to mean 'reputation' [IV 110]. To her, Belinda's honour is irretrievably lost with the loss of her lock. The outward sign is all. The sylphs, for all their concern with appearances, seem genuinely interested in Belinda's innocence. The language of Ariel's warning suggests she will not *victim fall* [I 95] in spite of her warm desires because the sylphs can divert her attention with childish delights; *treat* and the *moving Toyshop of the Heart* (but see Note on the eighteenth-century meaning of 'toyshop'). She is a *tender maid*, poised between childhood and womanhood. Honour may be a matter of clinging to conventional rules until she is more experienced in the ways of men, and the presence of the sylphs could be a sign of her acceptance of these conventions. Protecting a dress and protecting virginity are equally matters of 'taking care'. Her position is delicate because her innocence and youth, as well as her warmth and beauty, are part of her attractiveness. In the midst of his tribute to Belinda's beauty at its most assured (when she issues forth upon the Thames) Pope slips in the single word *unfix'd* to describe her sprightly mind. *Unfixed* captures an essential quality of the sylphs, with their *fluid bodies* [II 62] and *colours that change* [II 68], able to assume *what shapes they please* [I 70]. Like them Belinda is physically radiant and like them her moods vary and her emotions flutter. You could see the changeable sylphs as symbolizing the delicate loveliness and fluctuating emotions of a young girl on the brink of sexual awakening.

One effect of the sylphs in the poem, the contribution they make to its glittering atmosphere, has already been discussed. (See Approaches pp. 79–80.) It is possible to regard them as fulfilling a further role in the poem, a symbolic role. Many critics share the feeling that the sylphs 'stand for' something besides the part they play in the narrative; that they act as images. Their essence is beautiful, amoral, irresponsible and alluring. Brower writes that they stand for *feminine honour, flirtation, courtship, the necessary rivalry of man and woman*. Brooks suggests that the sylphs represent Pope's attempt *to do justice to the intricacies of the feminine mind*. He sees them as symbols of honour, *as it actually functions, not honour as a dry abstraction*. Parkin, recognizing that their protection depends upon Belinda's acceptance of the rules of social convention, sees them as symbolizing *the triviality of Belinda's world*. Another view of them is as distractions which protect young girls from serious romantic engagements without their being aware. Fairer argues that they are *Pope's most powerful and sustained image for the imagination*, stressing that as the Goddess Belinda is created by the sylphs from the imaginative profusion and disorder of the toilette, so the poem arises from the colourful imagination of Pope. Maynard Mack considers them to be symbols of feminine charm, what he calls the *womanliness of woman*. Differing as these readings are, they share the same feeling that the sylphs integrate into the poem as symbols.

The game of cards

The game of Ombre which Belinda plays with the Baron and a third unidentified knight is somewhat like modern whist or bridge. Three players play nine rounds or 'tricks' and the winner is the one who takes the most tricks. To win, a player must either win five tricks against an opponent or four tricks if the two opposing players win three and two respectively. The basic rules are:

---

1 Remove from a deck of cards all eights, nines and tens, leaving forty cards.
2 Deal nine cards to each player and place the remaining cards face down in a pile.
3 When trumps are decided, players may exchange their weaker cards for those in the pile.
4 The player who declares trumps plays the first card.
5 Each player plays one card in turn and the strongest card wins the trick.

However, the strength of the cards differs from those in modern games. Belinda leads from her strongest to her weakest; the Ace of Spades is the strongest trump, then the two of Spades, then the Ace of Clubs, then the remaining trump suit in descending order down to the three of Spades. Red Aces are lower in value than any face card in their suit.

Activity

With the help of the Notes for III 27–98 on pp 47–9, see how many of the remaining spaces you can complete in the plan of the game, given below. Pope does not give us sufficient information to complete the plan entirely but it is possible to decide who wins each trick.

The Game of Cards

Trick	Belinda	The Baron	Lord Anon.	Winner
1	Ace of Spades	A lesser Spade	A lesser Spade	Belinda
2	Two of Spades			
3			Card of little value	
4				
5		Queen of Spades		
6				
7				
8				
9				

You may have found the exaggerated language of the mock-epic contest complex and inexplicable at first reading. Has the replaying of the card game in the above activity helped you to distinguish between words which are unusual because they belong to the terminology of eighteenth-century card games and those which are an imitation of the grand epic style? Even at his most exaggerated, Pope bases his parody on the real game being played by the contestants while subtly hinting that the game may not be only about who wins at cards.

Activity

Re-read III 47–100. Can you find words which are both mock-epic and a realistic description of the game of cards?

Discussion

The *sable Matadores* and *swarthy Moors* [47–48] *Asia's troops and Afric's sable sons* [82] refer to the black suits; the King of Spade's *manly leg* [57] and the King of Clubs' *globe* [74] reflect the way in which these figures are represented in their full-length pictures on the faces of the cards; the *verdant field* [52] and *level green* [80] are both the grassy sports arena and the green baize or velvet card table. Pope's attitude to the underlying nature of the contest is conveyed in asides (*oh shameful chance!*) [88] and in his description of Belinda's behaviour. Why does he emphasize that the blood forsakes her *virgin's* cheek; why make her exultation so excited?

The Cave of Spleen

The cave is filled with grotesque objects described so imaginatively that it has always been a favourite subject with illustrators of the poem. A selection of these illustrations, taken from different periods, appears on pages 118–120.

Activity

Compare the various illustrations. What strikes you about them? (You might like to consider the similarities and differences in the artists' choice of objects and how closely they follow the description in the poem.) Do any of the illustrations accord with your own view of the Cave?

Certain objects seem to catch the imagination of artists. The Goddess Spleen generally dominates the picture. Handmaids are always present (although in variable numbers) and living teapots, maids turned bottles and the talking pie (which changes from a goosepie to a gooseberry pie over the years). Beardsley has a strange interpretation of *Men prove with child* as he delicately outlines a foetus in the swollen belly of one of his male figures (in the lower left-hand corner of the illustration) and in the thigh of the other. (See p. 120.) The sexual implication of the maids who call for men to cork their bottles is illustrated by Du Guernier (a contemporary artist whose illustrations were presumably approved by Pope) by placing men's heads in the bottles. (See p. 118.) By contrast, Wale, in 1757, has female heads in his bottles and later illustrators, like Beardsley, tend to avoid the problem altogether. (See p. 119.) Pope's couplet:

Unnumber'd throngs on ev'ry side are seen,
Of bodies chang'd to various forms by Spleen.   [IV 47–48]

invites artists to fill the Cave with their own imaginary grotesques. Beardsley in particular takes advantage of this. At the centre of his Cave, he places a recognizable portrait of Pope, copied from a well-known portrait by Kneller. This may be a tribute to the poem's author, or perhaps an acknowledgement that Pope himself suffered greatly from headaches and knew all too well the melancholy which arises from pain and sickness.

Whatever their differences in style and interpretation, the artists all strive to capture the atmosphere of diseased disorders which the Cave exudes. As images of abnormal procreation, repressed sexuality, neurotic anxiety and frustration the deformed objects in the Cave present an unappealing picture of a life in the *Gnomes embrace* [I 80]. Are we to take the peevish, ill-natured, affected women depicted here as a serious warning of what life could be like for Belinda? And does this fate lie in wait for her if, like Thalestris who basically rejects sex, she becomes a Prude, or if, like the nymphs *too conscious of their face* [I 79], she becomes too proud, or is it the inevitable consequence of old age? All these possibilities are hinted at by the contrast between the underworld of the Cave of Spleen and the golden, glittering beauty of Belinda's daylight environment.

Spleen was a recognized disease at the time with a long medical history pertaining to both men and women. It is noticeable that in Pope's Cave it is mainly women who are affected by it. Are we seeing the disease, a form of hysteria and depression created by repression and despair, from a male point of view which relates it primarily to female sexual disorders, or do you feel that Pope sympathizes with the choices which face beautiful young virgins? Belinda suffers *anxious cares* and *secret passions* [IV 1–2] and exactly what these are is not spelt out. Her passions may be *secret* because she barely understands them (her innocence is contrasted throughout the poem with the Baron's greater awareness of the underlying, sexual nature of the *game* they play). They may be *secret* because they relate to fears which Pope does not intend to probe although he sympathizes with the female situation.

If the Cave of Spleen helps to alert the reader to the tensions Belinda faces it does so without loss of lightness of tone. The grotesque objects are humorously presented, like nursery-book or fairy-tale transformations. The various illustrations catch the air of theatrical unreality in Pope's description which refuses to take anything in the Cave over-seriously.

Belinda

Through whose eyes do we see Belinda awakening? (We might ask the same question of the toilette.) Pope's? An implied male viewer's? How do these glimpses of private, intimate moments affect our view of Belinda?

As she drowsily and reluctantly awakens Belinda seems very human. Of course she is pampered; protected by her wealth in a world where *wretches hang*, but she is also a young girl dreaming romantic dreams. By the end of the first Canto however she has been transformed into a Goddess. She emerges at the start of Canto II adorned, adored and divine.

Activity

What techniques does Pope use to suggest that Belinda is divine?

Discussion

There seem to me to be at least four ways by which this is established. First, the female sex is regarded with reverence throughout the poem. Hailed as *the Fair* [II 91] and *Angel-like ador'd* [V 12], they are guided through the world by attendant sylphs [I 91–92]. Secondly, from these nymphs Belinda is especially singled out as the *Fairest of mortals*, the *distinguish'd care* of the bright inhabitants of air [I 27]. Thirdly, imagery confers upon her life-giving, divine power. From the moment of her awakening she is associated with the sun, the tim'rous *Sol* [I 13]. Three times in the first paragraph of Canto II she is compared to the sun and Pope claims that she equals him in glory. The gazers depend upon her for life-giving sustenance [II 13]; the gaiety of the world derives from her smile [II 52]. Finally we, the readers, witness the moment of her transformation.

Belinda's toilette is the climax of Canto I. Indeed it is one of the climaxes of the poem. It is organized into three sections, starting at

And now . . . Unnumber'd treasures . . . Now awful Beauty . . . [I 121–148] and each section uses a cluster of images to exemplify its central action.

Activity

What is happening in each section? Can you identify a phrase or an image cluster which sums up the action?

Discussion

The first section (see notes on Canto I 121–128) shows Belinda seated at her dressing table admiring herself in the mirror. This simple action is presented as an epic parody and as an act of religious worship. The phrase *sacred rites of Pride* seems to me a central image from which the other images flow. They are all taken from the ritual of worship; like an inner shrine the *Toilet* is *unveil'd* and the words of devotion continue: *mystic order, rob'd in white, adores, Cosmetic pow'rs, heav'nly Image, inferior Priestess, altar's side.* Belinda is both Priestess and Goddess, worshipping herself in a *rite of Pride.*

The second section (see notes on Canto I 129–138) lists the objects on her dressing table and the central image seems to me to be *glitt'ring spoil.* The world has been ransacked to adorn Belinda and the imagery of this section relates back to the idea of spoil. However conscious we are of the diminishing effect of the epic parallel (see note on Canto I 132), the tone does not seem entirely mocking. *India's glowing gems . . . all Arabia breathes* lend a radiance to Belinda's beauty which enchants and the array of her dressing table seems to be gifts for a Goddess. Some commentators on the poem believe that Pope came to mock his subject but stayed to adore. Others have suggested that the lines reflect the glow of eighteenth-century male pride in Belinda as a created object of desire because she is *deck'd* in the fruits of their mercantile success. The richer her decoration, the richer their prize. (For a discussion of this view see Approaches pp. 81–3.)

In the third section (see notes on Canto I 139–148) Belinda is made-up and her hair and gown are arranged. The effect of imagery may be less apparent here until you consider the verbs: *puts on, rises, repairs, awakens, calls forth, arise, quicken*. These are all words of creation. Belinda is born anew, transformed by the sylphs from a natural girl into a Goddess who will rival the sun. Is her beauty natural or acquired? The verbs *awakens* and *calls forth* suggest that her latent good looks are merely heightened by make-up but *purer blush* and *quicken* suggest that the sylphs have added something which did not previously exist.

She reigns, a Queen commanding her troops, until the Baron cuts off her lock. How does she behave then? she *screams* [III 156], she *shrieks* [III 157], she collapses into *tears* [IV 144]. With drooping head she sighs for *my best, my fav'rite curl* [IV 148]. Does this sound like a Goddess grieving or a retreat into childishness? At the end of Canto V the sun image appears again, this time to spell out the truth of Belinda's situation. She is human, not divine. She may, in the lightweight language of coquetry, slay *millions* but in reality her *fair suns shall set*.

The movement of the poem can be read as an elevation leading to a fall. *Thy own importance know* the sylphs urged, and pride betrays Belinda into believing that her power is limitless. The toilette which transformed her was called *the rites of Pride*. At times the language echoes Milton, recalling Satan and Eve and the Biblical Fall. Mirroring this, Belinda's pride changes to despair and her guardianship moves from the sylphs to the gnomes. Belinda appears privileged but fragile. At what cost, at what effort her beauty is maintained. Is fear the underlying reality of Belinda's world, fear of a fall, fear of growing old, of growing ugly, of losing the power to attract men? Is the fragility of her world the result of tension and anxiety engendered by the losing battle with time? She strives to keep up appearances and nature and youth are on her side but this will not always be so. As Belinda's *glories* come under attack, her passion and panic mount. Do you find her less attractive towards the end of the poem?

Prudes and coquettes

Coquettes charm and conquer men while refusing to capitulate to them and this possibility is open to Belinda. Her attractions are manifest but her petticoat is a *seven-fold fence*. Does she seek to retain power over men by remaining unavailable, the *wise man's passion, and the vain man's toast*? The Cave of Spleen hints that the end of a coquette's existence is *Affectation*, the vain striving to maintain power once beauty has fled.

Prudes on the other hand retain their independence from men by disdaining the sexual battle altogether. *Ill-Nature* may personify their final position. Thalestris encourages Belinda to retrieve at all costs the sign of her dishonour and retreat into prudery. Are these Belinda's only options? Her predicament can be seen more clearly perhaps if you ask yourself the question, Do you expect Belinda to marry one day or do you feel the poem suggests it is equally likely that she will live the life of an old maid? Is Pope presenting these alternatives in an even-handed manner or does the language of the poem show that he favours one of them?

Clarissa's speech is often taken as stating Pope's position, although there are many other intepretations of it. (See general note on Canto V 1–34). It can be read as the tactical compromise of common sense; worldly, well-meant advice on how to keep a man. It can be seen as answering Belinda's anxieties that there will be loss if she gives way to her desires, a loss imaged in the stains and cracks which so concern the sylphs. It could be an attempt to redefine for contemporary women a concept of honour which applied to male epic heroes. In the world of belles, honour becomes the courage to face decay with good humour and a duty to *use* the power of beauty *well*, although what is meant by that phrase is left for the reader to decide. To the sylphs honour means purity whether in a vase, a dress or a woman. Beauty must be flawless and they admit of no discrepancy between appearance and reality. To Thalestris and the Baron honour means reputation, the outward sign. Does Clarissa offer a third definition – honour as the acceptance of male domination with good humour and as patience instead of despair before the inevitability of change?

If so, this draws attention to feminist readings which see Belinda as diminished by her experiences, moving from an independent girl to one more willing to accept the limitations of society. Such readings regard the poem as dominated by a male point of view in spite of Belinda being the subject. In this interpretation women become objects for men's use, trophies or commodities, and they are judged as using their power (beauty or sex) *well* when they accept gracefully the social place which has been defined for them by men. You may feel that Pope shows more sympathy with the position of women in eighteenth-century society than this view allows but it is worth thinking about the extent to which Belinda's power is dictated by the willingness of men to be attracted.

Transformations

Activity

Can you think of things in the poem which are transformed?

Discussion

There are mock-epic transformations when Gods dwindle into sylphs and heroes become little men. Conversely, ordinary things are enlarged. Cups become China's earth, a comb becomes ivory and all Arabia is contained in a box of perfume. There are the changes brought about by the natural passage of time as dresses are stained and curled locks turn to grey. In the Cave of Spleen there are unnatural changes; maids are bewitched into bottles, age becomes eighteen and men become women. There are the elevating changes; girls are raised to goddesses and a lock is transformed to a star.

Is change for better or for worse? Cracked china and flawed jars suggest that Belinda's loss of virginity is a real loss, a flaw in her beauty. But beauty would inevitably decay. There are messages in the theme of change. How you read them depends upon what you believe the poem celebrates, Belinda's virginal beauty or her acceptance of womanhood.

Does anything in the poem remain stable; does anything last? If the lock survives (and it will outlast all the characters in the poem) it does so by the art of Pope's poetry, by the power of the Muse. Some commentators suggest that Pope is attracted to disorder and the imaginative profusion of Belinda's dressing table because of its energy and vitality. They see it as an image of creativity. From chaos a Goddess is created, as, at the end, there must be loss to achieve gain. The apotheosis of the lock would not have taken place had Belinda stayed at home or followed Clarissa's advice to accept her loss with good humour. What do you think of this view?

The style of the poem

Structure

When Pope set out to please Caryll by writing something to 'laugh them together again' he chose to write a mock-epic and this decision determined the style of his poem. Even the first version of the *Rape* which lacks many of the epic parallels he was to add in later versions is mock-epic in language and in tone. The five-canto version however follows more closely the structure of the epic.

You may find that you prefer the original version which is printed in Appendix 2. With fewer mock-epic incidents, the narrative line is clearer, the pace quicker and the jokes more obvious to twentieth-century readers who may lack the background to recognize classical allusions with ease. The greatest change, the introduction of the sylphs, fits so deftly into the five-canto poem that it is astonishing to think they had not been imagined from the start. Could you have told from reading only the five-Canto poem which lines were the additions? The poem builds to the same climaxes, the public appearance of Belinda, the severing of her lock, the battle for its repossession and the final apotheosis. The additional incidents, the Toilette, the Game of Cards and the Cave of Spleen, allow Pope to extend, expand and thus deepen the implications of his story. At what cost or gain he does this depends upon your response to the different versions.

Within the poem the structure of the paragraphs creates and reinforces the climaxes. Consider, for example, the closing paragraph of Canto III. The tone is declamatory and epic, set by the grandly (but vaguely) expressed subject, *What Time wou'd spare*, and the reversed syntax of *from Steel receives*. The build-up continues with repetition of phrases and grammatical structures until the paragraph culminates in a mocking deflation of Belinda for imagining that her lock could outlast the towers of Troy. Yet the declamatory tone is held in the resounding final line. Is Belinda enlarged by the mock-epic comparison? Or is she diminished by it?

Clearer examples of how Pope builds his paragraphs towards deflating conclusions are probably Canto I 121–148 and Canto III 1–8. You might like to look at these and consider the effect of their closing couplets. At what point does the tone change from epic to conversational? Is the joke at the end heightened by the build-up which precedes it? Once recognized, you will begin to register further instances of Pope building paragraphs by these methods towards mocking conclusions.

Some paragraphs move in the opposite direction. Consider Canto III 147–154 or Canto V 103–112. Starting in the tone of the eighteenth-century drawing-room they end in high epic style. Do the lighter lines make a joke of the concluding couplets or does an echo of the epic lend dignity and pathos to the concluding lines?

Language

Pope uses the standard epic formula of a noun accompanied by an adjective which is elevated and inexact in meaning. A favourite translation of a phrase which occurs repeatedly in the *Iliad* is *wine-dark sea*. Virgil associates his hero with the Latin adjective 'pius' and refers to him constantly as *pius Aeneas*. It is easy to find examples of Pope using this feature of epic style from *dire offense* and *mighty contests* to *verdant fields and smoaking tyde*.

Pope himself laughed at the familiar formula in *The Art of Sinking* where he called it *periphrase* (which means a round-about way of saying something) or a:

> Manner of expressing a known Idea, which should be so misteriously couch'd, as to give the Reader the Pleasure of guessing what it is that the Author can possibly mean: and a surprise when he finds it.

The Rape is full of phrases where what is intended by the adjective is slightly mysterious: *secret passions, grateful liquors, two-edg'd weapon, fatal shears*. The choice of inflated words and the association of nouns with adjectives grand in tone and vague in meaning are features of the epic and its derivative, the mock-epic. In the mock-epic there is shock as well as surprise when one realizes what the phrase means because the unimportance of the object is highlighted by the grandiose ring of the phrase which describes it. A *two-edg'd weapon* sounds ferocious until one remembers that it is a pair of scissors so tiny that the Baron can hardly fit them on his fingers' ends.

The mock-epic joke lies partly in the imbalance between description and what is being described and partly in sudden linguistic transitions which, without altering the epic formula, juxtapose phrases recalling the high ideals of the epic world (*mighty hearts, important charge, sharp vengeance, dire event*) with phrases which in their colloquial, frivolous, chatty tone belong clearly in the world of the Eighteenth century; *elemental Tea, downy pillow, winning lips, midnight masquerades, young Coquettes, hidden blush*, *giddy circle*, *tender maid*, *gentle Damon*, *tender Billet-doux*, *burning chocolate*, *fav'rite Lock*, *wretched Sylph*. Epic grandeur is always on the brink of being undercut by the familiar and intimate accents of contemporary gossip.

The heroic couplet: rhythm and rhyme

The Rape is written in the rhythm of the iambic pentameter. Each line has five feet and each foot consists of two syllables, the second of which is stressed. As this amounts to ten syllables in a line, the rhythm is also known as decasyllabic. A rhymed pair of iambic pentameters is called a heroic couplet and this is the style in which Pope wrote *The Rape*.

Pope's rhymes tend on the whole to be monosyllabic: *glade/shade*; *breeze/trees*; *glides/tydes*; *fled/dead*; *found/wound*; *strain/pain*; *must/dust*; *fame/name*. Taken out of context, many have an epic tone. Amidst these expected rhymes Pope slips in ones which lower the tone, mocking and undercutting the epic mode; *mankind/behind*; *bestow/Furbelow*; *brocade/masquerade*; *note/petticoat*; *fail/whale*. These tend to be polysyllabic which creates a lighter tone but the joke also lies in the oddity of the pairing and the inventiveness of the rhyme. You might like to look at other couplets and consider for yourself the effect of Pope's rhymes.

The same movement of building towards a deflating climax which we saw Pope using in his paragraphs appears in many of the couplets. He often overturns an apparently straightforward meaning by a twist in the couplet's tail. Look, for instance, at this couplet:

> While fish in streams, or birds delight in air,
> Or in a Coach and six the *British* Fair. (III 163–64]

The tone of both lines is the same: lightweight, unserious. The first line describes Nature delighting in essential life-giving elements and the second line describes the fashionable set delighting in the show of wealth. The closeness of the comparison is increased by the rhyme which yokes these examples of delight. Yet the juxtaposition is unsettling. There is a qualitative difference between the natural enjoyment of being alive and the self-satisfied enjoyment of luxurious fashion which carries a implicit judgement on the British Fair. Similarly,

> Whether the nymph shall break *Diana's* law,
> Or some frail *China* jar receive a flaw. [II 105–106]

The two disasters are ironically contrasted and the irony is created by the deceiving nature of the couplet. The two events are closely linked by rhyme and by the couplet structure which allots them one line apiece, apparently awarding them equal weight. The surprise comes when we realize the accidental nature of the second event and we are left wondering about nymphs who view Diana's law as a matter of accident. Is this a joke or a judgement? The closeness of comparison is increased by the seemingly parallel phrases *the nymph shall break* and *some frail China jar receive* and the subtle difference between them. The first phrase has an active verb and the second a passive one.

Many of the most cutting couplets follow this pattern, an apparently complimentary or neutral first line reversed by the implications of the second line. Statements are called in question by ironic undertones, twists of meaning which surprise by their unexpected wit and acerbity. The reverse can occur in a phrase, as in:

> Now lap-dogs give themselves the rousing shake,
> And sleepless lovers, just at twelve, awake. [I 15–16]

Where the phrase *just at twelve* throws a questioning light on the *sleepless* lovers. It can be created by a single, deftly-placed word. what is the effect of *unfix'd* in the following couplet?

> Her lively looks a sprightly mind disclose,
> Quick as her eyes, and as unfix'd as those. [II 9–10]

There are many other moments in the poem where you will recognize Pope turning the couplet to his satiric purposes. Perhaps the deflation is nowhere more apparent than in the *double-entendres*. Consider the implications of the closing of the couplets IV 175–176, V 77–78 and V 97–98.

The iambic pentameter and the closing of each couplet with a rhyme mean that Pope is writing in a highly restrictive mode. The formal restraints of his chosen style mirror the world of artifice and decorum which his poem describes. Like the china jar, the flowered brocade and the trembling sylphs, his couplets are held in a delicate state of poise and tension which cannot be broken without damage. In passion and anger, Belinda and the Baron may overstep the bounds, but Pope's couplets never falter. In this assured control lies much of the wit and charm of the poem.

Zeugma

Zeugma is the technical term given to a device Pope uses frequently in *The Rape*. A single verb governs two objects and is used in a different sense in each case, for example in the comment that great ANNA *Dost sometimes counsel take—and sometimes Tea* [III 8], where advice and a cup of tea are both proper objects of the verb 'to take' but read incongruously when used at the same time. Or in the description of Sir Plume who *first the snuff-box open'd, then the case* [IV 126], where again it is grammatically correct to open both a snuff-box and a legal case but it sounds oddly awry when the phrases are set so closely together. One effect of this device is to add to the humorous atmosphere of the poem. There is a quirkiness which puzzles and delights as we sense the solution almost at the moment of hesitant misunderstanding.

In other ways, however, Pope's use of zeugma seems to go to the heart of his mocking and ambiguous attitude towards Belinda and reflects his judgement of her world. There is a sense that, if not to the reader then at least to the subjects of the lines quoted, ANNA and Sir Plume, the incongruously different objects are of equal importance. If Queen Anne takes counsel in the spirit in which she drinks tea, what does this imply about the seriousness with which she treats state business?

Activity

Think about the effect of Pope's use of zeugma in the following lines:

Or stain her honour, or her new brocade,   [II 107]
Or lose her heart, or necklace, at a ball;   [II 109]

Discussion

What strikes me first is the unexpectedness of the things lost and stained, or rather the amusing unexpectedness of their conjunction. Is Ariel not right to feel that any of these mishaps would be upsetting? And yet it seems ridiculous to equate them as the grammar and the satisfying sound of the neatly balanced lines suggests. If one searches for the sense of disturbance where it appears to lie, in the meaning of the lines, is Pope's attitude any clearer? Are we to take the juxtaposition as a joke; as an ironic comment upon the moral disorder of the poem's characters; as a judgement on a world which values fashion and entertainment as the business of life? Or are we to see it as a sympathetic response to virginal belles whose beauty is as precious and as delicate as a china jar and whose sexual attractiveness requires both exposure and protection? You may have found yet another reading of these elusive lines. The ambiguity of zeugma opens up multiple possibilities.

Image Patterns

The use of imagery, for example in the depiction of the sylphs, has been discussed at various points in the Notes and Approaches. I want to look more closely at three image patterns in the poem. The first is the use of the word *lapdogs*. Belinda possesses an adored lapdog, Shock, and many of the references are to him; waking her in the morning [I 115–116], guarded by Ariel [II 116], vainly trying to warn her against leaving for Hampton Court [IV 164]. Canto I 15–16 associates lovers with lap-dogs and in Canto III there is the claim:

> Not louder shrieks to pitying heav'n are cast,
> When husbands or when lapdogs breathe their last; [III 157–158]

The references can be read, as they are surely intended to be, as jokes. Is there an underlying sense that the emotions of young girls and wives are directed towards lapdogs in place of lovers and husbands? Shock could be an image for the affections Belinda will feel when her passions, as yet unfixed, centre on a single, chosen man.

Another image in the poem is formed by the noun clusters, the lists of oddly random, assorted things: the confusion and profusion on Belinda's dressing table; the things lost on earth and treasured in the lunar sphere; Thalestris' list of beauty aids; unnumbered things in the Cave of Spleen; the Baron's love offerings. They share the quality of being jackdaw collections. They seem to operate like a symbol, imaging the arbitrary possessiveness of the material world of beaux and belles who cannot distinguish between virginity and vases, necklaces and hearts, lovers and lapdogs, between honour as outward show and honour as an ideal.

The sun is probably the clearest example of an image which pervades the poem and helps to carry its themes. Throughout, the reader knows that the claim that Belinda rivals or eclipses the sun must be false and that knowledge is one of the jokes against her. Unlike Belinda, we are surely never meant to take it as a serious parallel. The power of poetry, *the Muse*, gives Belinda what physical beauty could not, enduring fame with her name inscribed *'midst the stars*. Which of us would remember Arabella Fermor if Pope had not written a poem about her lock?

The lock is transformed into a star and we sense that this will last, a lesser luminary than Belinda herself but a permanent one. Recognition of the transience of Belinda's beauty lies at the heart of Pope's teasing use of the sun image. The poem closes with the reality that *those fair suns*, her eyes, *must set*. Even as one light is dimmed, another rises. There always was an eternal sphere in which things were rightly valued. The lock takes its place beyond the *Lunar sphere*, the lower world inhabited by the sylphs, in the *heav'ns*. The power of poetry lifts it to a lasting fame. Sun and star represent the firm, sure world which lies beyond the world of Belinda and the sylphs.

Other times: other views

The *Rape* has not always been admired. The artificiality of its setting and the apparent triviality of its subject have led to periods when it has not been widely favoured, but there has been a steady chorus of appreciation across the years and, at present, Pope's reputation stands high. Here is a selection of comments by readers over the last two hundred years. Do any of them express your feelings about the poem?

'In this work are exhibited, in a very high degree, the two most engaging powers of an author. New things are made familiar, and familiar things are made new.'

Samuel Johnson 1781

'It is made of gauze and silver spangles. The most glittering appearance is given to everything, to paste, pomatum, billet-doux, and patches. Airs, languid airs, breathe around:- the atmosphere is perfumed with affectation.'

William Hazlitt 1818

'The criticism the poem provides is sometimes more a picture than a criticism. It is so elaborate, shifting, constellated, that the intellect is baffled and demoralised by the aesthetic sense and emotions.'

Geoffrey Tillotson 1940

'Belinda's charm is not viewed uncritically, but the charm is real; it can survive the poet's knowledge of how much art and artifice have gone into making up the charm . . .

Pope is too clear-sighted to allow that the charming Belinda is merely the innocent victim of a rude assault. Why has she cherished the lock at all? In part at least "to the destruction of mankind", though mankind, of course, in keeping with the convention, wishes so to be destroyed. Pope suggests that the Baron may even be the victim rather than the aggressor – it is a moot question whether he has seized the lock or been ensnared by it . . . After all, does not Belinda want the Baron (and young men in general) to covet the lock? She certainly does not want to retain possession of the lock for ever.'

Cleanth Brooks 1943

'Pope presents the absurdities of the fashionable world with affection, and with an eye to the delicate beauties that its best graces unfold. But he never allows us to forget that it is also a world whose ethical judgements are in sad disarray. Hearts and necklaces, lap-dogs and lovers, statesmanship and tea, queens and Indian screens, the hunger of jurymen and justice, Bibles and billets-doux: the verse of the poem entangles these trifles and values together in order to reflect a similar entanglement in this society's mind.'

Maynard Mack 1950

'We begin to see that Belinda's presentation of herself as an object originates in her society's reduction of all value to money value, all life to commodity . . . The right use of beauty is not to tease a man, but to catch a man: a husband is "what beauty gains".'

Sheila Delany 1975

'Eroticism suffuses the poem like a sea, quite appropriately considering its subject, but the insistent delicacy of its strategy calls for a similar delicacy in the reader.'

Maynard Mack 1985

'Pope treats Belinda's cosmetic arts . . . as Beauty's Arms – a kind of chastity belt designed to protect Belinda from not for the Baron. The coquette's conscious intention has never been to relinquish her place in the sun to him. In terms of the unwinding of Belinda's built-in destiny as a woman, however, the answer to Thalestris' question (Was it for this you took such constant care . . .?) is flatly 'Yes'. To shine for man's sake – or to reflect his light – is woman's trial on earth, and Pope has designed his heroine to symbolize this fact.'

Ellen Pollak 1985

Chronology

Events in Pope's life

1688	Pope born in London.
1700	Pope's family move from London to Binfield perhaps to escape the ten-mile law against Catholics.
1705	Pope begins to visit London and meet with literary men.

Other events

1679–81	The Exclusion crisis. The Whig party make several attempts to pass a bill in Parliament excluding the Roman Catholic James, Duke of York, from the succession.
1685	Death of Charles II and accession of James II.
1688	Flight of James II to France. William of Orange lands in England.
1689	Accession of William and Mary.
1701	The Act of Settlement provides for a Protestant heir to the English throne. The Pretender is recognized by Louis XIV. England at war with France.
1702	Death of William and accession of Anne.
1704	Marlborough defeats the French at the Battle of Blenheim.

Year	Historical events	Year	Pope's life and works
1707	Union of England and Scotland.	1709	Pope's early poems published in Tonson's *Miscellanies*
		1711	Pope's *Essay on Criticism* published.
		1712	*The Rape of the Locke* written.
1713	Peace treaty concluded with France.		
1714	Death of Anne and accession of George I.	1714	The enlarged version of *The Rape of the Lock* published
1715	Jacobite rebellion.	1715	Pope starts publishing his translation of the *Iliad*.
		1717	Clarissa's speech added to *The Rape of the Lock*.
		1718	Pope and his mother move to Twickenham.
1720	South Sea Bubble scandal.		
1721	Walpole becomes Lord Treasurer.		
1727	Death of George I and accession of George II.		
		1728	Pope's *Dunciad* published.
		1731	*Moral Essay IV* published.
		1733	*Moral Essay III* published.
		1734	*Moral Essay I* and *Essay on Man* published.
		1735	*Epistle to Arbuthnot* and *Moral Essay II* published.
1739	England at war with Spain.		
		1743	*The Dunciad* published (with an additional book).
		1744	Pope dies.
1745	Jacobite rebellion.		

Further Reading

Editions

Alexander Pope, *The Rape of the Lock and Other Poems*, ed. Geoffrey Tillotson, Methuen, 1940.

Life

Mack, Maynard. *Alexander Pope: A Life*, Yale University Press, 1985.

Books

Brower, R. A., *Alexander Pope: The Poetry of Allusion*, Oxford, 1959. This contains a useful chapter on the classical background of the poem. This chapter is printed in its entirety in *Hunt*. See Collections of Articles below.

Brown, Laura, *Alexander Pope*, Basil Blackwell, 1985. A Marxist reading of the poem which considers the classical allusions as images of economic imperialism.

Cunningham, J. S., *Pope: the Rape of the Lock*, Edward Arnold, 1961. A stimulating introduction to the poem.

Fairer, David, *Pope's Imagination*, Manchester University Press, 1984. This contains a chapter discussing the sylphs as a symbol of the imagination.

Hammond, Brean, *Pope* Harvester, 1986. This has a chapter on Pope's poems about women which takes account of feminist readings.

Jones, J. A., *Pope's Couplet Art*, Ohio U. P., Athens, Ohio, 1969. This gives a detailed analysis of Pope's use of the couplet form.

Rogers, Pat, *An Introduction to Pope*, Methuen, 1975. A lively introduction to the poem.

Collections of Articles

Barnard, J. (ed.), *Pope: The Critical Heritage*, London and Boston, 1973. This reprints historical responses to the poem.

Hunt, J. D. (ed.), *The Rape of the Lock: A Casebook*, Macmillan, 1968. This contains some of the best essays on the poem published in the Nineteenth and early Twentieth centuries.

Mack, Maynard, (ed.), *Essential Articles for the Study of Alexander Pope*, Archon Books, Hamden, Conn., 1968. This contains some of the articles reprinted in *Hunt*.

Mack, Maynard, (ed.), *Pope: Recent Essays by Several Hands*, Archon, Hamden, Conn., 1980. This has essays by W. K. Wimsatt on the Game of Cards, by Earl R. Wasserman on allusions and by Louis A. Landa on the economic background.

Rousseau G. S. (ed.), *Twentieth-Century Interpretations of The Rape of the Lock*, Prentice-Hall, Englewood Cliffs, N. J., 1969. This also contains many of the essays reprinted in *Hunt*.

Additional Articles

Delany, Sheila, 'Sex and Politics in Pope's Rape of the Lock', *English Studies in Canada*, 1975. A reading which explores both feminist and Marxist readings.

Kenner, Hugh, 'Pope's Reasonable Rhymes', *E. L. H. 41*, 1974. A detailed analysis of Pope's use of rhyme.

Landa, Louis, 'Pope's Belinda, The General Emporie of the World, and the Wondrous Worm', *Essays in Eighteenth Century Literature*, 1980. A reading which focuses upon the poem's economic setting.

Pollak, Ellen, 'Rereading The Rape of the Lock', *Studies in Eighteenth-Century Culture 10, 1981*. A feminist reading of the poem.

Tasks

1 'Beauty draws us with a single hair.' Identify the ways in which Pope creates a sense of Belinda's beauty for the reader and the complexity of his attitude towards her.

2 In the final analysis do you find the poem's attitude towards Belinda mocking or sympathetic?

3 'She has got herself up to hunt, to prey, to capture, and her object is not love itself but the social status that comes from being admired.' To what extent do you find this criticism of Belinda just?

4 If you were Arabella Fermor would you have felt flattered by Pope's portrayal of Belinda?

5 Thalestris refers to Belinda's lock as *th'inestimable prize*. How does Pope create a sense of the lock's value and why do you think it is so prized?

6 The Baron has been called both aggressor and a victim. Do you agree strongly with either term, or do you find your sympathy for him changes in the course of reading the poem?

7 'The most glittering appearance is given to everything . . . the atmosphere is perfumed with affectation.' Do you agree with Hazlitt's statement? How is the atmosphere of the poem created?

8 Draw your own picture of the sylphs. Accompany it with an account of the details from the poem which it illustrates. Were there elements in Pope's description which you felt could not be captured in your drawing?

9 Choose one section from the poem which you find amusing and show how it exemplifies Pope's wit.

10 By close analysis of selected examples, show how the exaggerated contrasts implied by the mock-heroic style add to the humour of the poem.

11 What do you feel that you have learned about life in eighteenth-century London from reading *The Rape of the Lock*?

12 Choose a section from the poem which at first sight presented you with difficulties but which on further study you have come to enjoy. Describe your earlier difficulties and what it is that you now find enjoyable in the passage.

13 Compose a paragraph of heroic couplets to describe items likely to lie on a teenager's dressing table today. Try to catch Pope's light-hearted tone of affectionate mockery.

14 Do you find Clarissa's advice wise or worldy-wise?

Belinda embarking for Hampton Court, surrounded by
cherubic sylphs, 'fair nymphs' and 'well-drest youth'. An
eighteenth-century watercolour by Thomas Stothard

Belinda at her toilette, with Shock, Ariel, fairy sylphs and
a bat-like creature, perhaps escaped from the Cave of
Spleen. An unsigned nineteenth-century sketch, probably
by Benjamin West or William Locke

An eighteenth-century print of the Royal Exchange in the City of London. See Canto III 23

A manteau, pinned up at the back in the fashion of the time to reveal an underskirt or petticoat. See Canto II 118 and Canto IV 8

117

The Cave of Spleen by Du Guernier, one of the etchings
which illustrated the 1714 edition of *The Rape of the Lock*.

The hand maidens, Affectation and Ill-nature, attend
the Goddess Spleen, while sooty Umbriel flits through the
mist above living teapots and bottles corked with men's
heads

The Cave of Spleen by Samuel Wale, an etching from the
1757 edition of Pope's collected *Works*.

Ill-nature and Affectation stand behind the Goddess, with
Pain at her side and Megrim at her head. Umbriel hovers
above a living teapot, bottles corked with maids' heads and
pie through whose crust poke a head and webbed goose foot

The Cave of Spleen by Aubrey Beardsley, a photogravure
illustration to *The Rape of the Lock* (1896).

Umbriel and the Goddess Spleen dominate this gathering of
fantastical creatures (some not mentioned in the poem). Along
the lower edge stand pregnant men, living teapots and a tiny
gooseberry pie, while in the centre is a portrait of Pope

Appendix 1

Before Pope published his second, fuller version of the poem in 1714 he offered two alternative introductions to Arabella Fermor for her approval. She chose the prose dedication which has traditionally accompanied the poem ever since. This little poem was published anonymously in 1717 in a miscellany which Pope edited and later editors of his works believe that it is the discarded introduction to *The Rape of the Lock*.

To BELINDA on the *RAPE OF THE LOCK*

Pleas'd in these lines, *Belinda*, you may view
How things are priz'd, which once belong'd to you.
If on some meaner head this Lock had grown,
The nymph despis'd, the Rape had been unknown.
But what concerns the valiant and the fair,
The Muse asserts as her peculiar care.
Thus *Helens* Rape and *Menelaus'* wrong
Became the Subject of great *Homer's* song;
And, lost in ancient times, the golden fleece
10 Was rais'd to fame by all the wits of *Greece*.

Had fate decreed, propitious to your pray'rs,
To give their utmost date to all your hairs;
This Lock, of which late ages now shall tell,
Had dropt like fruit, neglected, when it fell.

Nature to your undoing arms mankind
With strength of body, artifice of mind;
But gives your feeble sex, made up of fears,
No guard but virtue, no redress but tears.
Yet custom (seldom to your favour gain'd)
20 Absolves the virgin when by force constrain'd
Thus *Lucrece* lives unblemish'd in her fame,
A bright example of young *Tarquin's* shame.
Such praise is yours – and such shall you possess.
Your virtue equal, tho' your loss be less.
Then smile Belinda at reproachful tongues,
Still warm our hearts, and still inspire our songs.
But would your charms to distant times extend,
Let *Jervas* paint them, and let *Pope* commend.
Who censure most, more precious hairs would lose,
30 To have the *Rape* recorded by his Muse.

Appendix 2

The first version of the poem, published in 1712.

THE RAPE of the LOCKE
An Heroi-comical POEM

> *Nolueram,* Belinda, *tuos violare capillos,*
> *Sed juvat hoc precibus me tribuisse tuis.*
> MART. Lib. 12. Ep. 86.

Canto I

What dire Offence from Am'rous causes springs,
What mighty Quarrels rise from Trivial Things,
I sing – this verse to C———l, Muse! is due;
This, ev'n *Belinda* may vouchsafe to view:
Slight is the subject, but not so the Praise,
If She inspire, and He approve my Lays.

Say what strange Motive, Goddess! cou'd compel
A well-bred *Lord* t'assault a gentle *Belle?*
Oh say what stranger Cause, yet unexplor'd,
10   Cou'd make a gentle *Belle* reject a *Lord?*
And dwells such Rage in *softest Bosoms* then?
And lodge such daring Souls in *Little Men?*

Sol thro' white Curtains did his Beams display,
And op'd those Eyes which brighter shine than they;
Shock just had giv'n himself the rowzing Shake,
And Nymphs prepar'd their *Chocolate* to take;
Thrice the wrought Slipper knock'd against the Ground,
And striking Watches the tenth Hour resound.

Belinda rose, and 'midst attending Dames
20   Launch'd on the Bosom of the silver *Thames*:
A Train of well-drest Youths around her shone,

And ev'ry Eye was fix'd on her alone.
On her white Breast a sparkling *Cross* she wore,
Which *Jews* might kiss, and Infidels adore.
Her lively Looks a sprightly Mind disclose,
Quick as her Eyes, and as unfixt as those:
Favours to none, to all she Smiles extends;
Oft she rejects, but never once offends.
Bright as the Sun her Eyes the Gazers strike,
30   And, like the Sun, they shine on all alike.
Yet graceful Ease, and Sweetness void of Pride,
Might hide her Faults, if *Belles* had Faults to hide:
If to her share some Female Errors fall,
Look on her Face, and you'll forgive 'em all.

   This Nymph, to the Destruction of Mankind,
Nourish'd two Locks, which graceful hung behind
In equal Curls, and well conspir'd to deck
With shining Ringlets the smooth Iv'ry Neck.
Love in these Labyrinths his Slaves detains,
40   And mighty Hearts are held in slender Chains.
With hairy Sprindges we the Birds betray,
Slight Lines of Hair surprize the Finny Prey,
Fair Tresses Man's Imperial Race insnare,
And Beauty draws us with a *single Hair*.

   Th'Advent'rous *Baron* the bright Locks admir'd,
He saw, he wish'd, and to the Prize aspir'd:
Resolv'd to win, he meditates the way,
By Force to ravish, or by Fraud betray;
For when Success a Lover's Toil attends,
50   Few ask, if Fraud or Force attain'd his Ends.

   For this, ere *Phœbus* rose, he had implor'd
Propitious Heav'n, and ev'ry Pow'r ador'd,
But chiefly *Love* – to *Love* an Altar built,
Of twelve vast *French* Romances, neatly gilt.
There lay the Sword-knot *Sylvia's* Hands had sown,
With *Flavia's* Busk that oft had rapp'd his own:
A fan, a Garter, half a Pair of Gloves;
And all the Trophies of his former Loves.

With tender *Billet-doux* he lights the Pyre,
60   And breathes three am'rous Sighs to raise the Fire,
Then prostrate falls, and begs with ardent Eyes
Soon to obtain, and long possess the Prize:
The Pow'rs gave Ear, and granted half his Pray'r,
The rest, the Winds dispers'd in empty Air.

Close by those Meads for ever crown'd with Flow'rs,
Where *Thames* with Pride surveys his rising Tow'rs,
There stands a Structure of Majestick Frame,
Which from the neighb'ring *Hampton* takes its Name.
Here *Britain's* Statesmen oft the Fall foredoom
70   Of foreign Tyrants, and of Nymphs at home;
Here Thou, great *Anna!* whom three Realms obey,
Dost sometimes Counsel take – and sometimes *Tea*.

Hither our Nymphs and Heroes did resort,
To taste awhile the Pleasures of a Court;
In various Talk the chearful hours they past,
Of, who was *Bitt*, or who *Capotted* last:
This speaks the glory of the *British Queen*,
And that describes a charming *Indian Screen*;
A third interprets Motions, Looks, and Eyes;
80   At ev'ry Word a Reputation dies.
Snuff, or the *Fan*, supply each Pause of Chatt,
With singing, laughing, ogling, and all that.

Now, when declining from the Noon of Day,
The Sun obliquely shoots his burning Ray;
When hungry Judges soon the Sentence sign,
And Wretches hang that Jury-men may Dine;
When Merchants from th'*Exchange* return in Peace,
And the long Labours of the *Toilette* cease—
The Board's with Cups and Spoons, alternate, crown'd;
90   The Berries crackle, and the mill turns round;
On shining Altars of *Japan* they raise
The silver *Lamp*; the fiery Spirits blaze;
From silver Spouts the grateful Liquors glide,
And *China's* earth receives the smoking Tyde:
At once they gratifie their Smell and Taste,

While frequent Cups prolong the rich Repast.
Coffee, (which makes the Politician wise,
And see thro' all things with his half-shut Eyes)
Sent up in Vapours to the *Baron's* Brain
100 New Stratagems, the radiant Locke to gain.
Ah cease, rash Youth! desist e'er 'tis too late,
Fear the just Gods, and think of *Scylla's* Fate!
Chang'd to a bird, and sent to flitt in Air,
She dearly pays for *Nisus'* injur'd Hair!

But when to Mischief Mortals bend their Mind,
How soon fit Instruments of Ill they find?
Just then, *Clarissa* drew with tempting Grace
A two-edg'd Weapon from her shining Case;
So Ladies in Romance assist their Knight,
110 Present the Spear, and arm him for the Fight.
He takes the Gift with rev'rence, and extends
The little Engine on his Finger's Ends,
This just behind *Belinda's* Neck he spread,
As o'er the fragrant Steams she bends her Head:
He first expands the glitt'ring *Forfex* wide
T'inclose the Lock; then joins it, to divide;
One fatal stroke the sacred Hair does sever
From the fair Head, for ever, and for ever!

The living Fires come flashing from her Eyes,
120 And Screams of Horror rend th'affrighted Skies.
Not louder Shrieks by Dames to Heav'n are cast,
When Husbands die, or *Lap-dogs* breath their last,
Or when rich *China* Vessels fal'n from high,
In glitt'ring Dust and painted Fragments lie!

Let Wreaths of triumph now my Temples twine,
(The Victor cry'd) the glorious Prize is mine!
While Fish in Streams, or Birds delight in Air,
Or in a Coach and Six the *British* Fair,
As long as *Atalantis* shall be read,
130 Or the small Pillow grace a Lady's Bed,
While *Visits* shall be paid on solemn Days,
When num'rous Wax-lights in bright Order blaze,

While Nymphs take Treats, or Assignations give,
So long my Honour, Name, and Praise shall live!

What Time wou'd spare, from Steel receives its date,
And Monuments, like Men, submit to Fate!
Steel did the labour of the Gods destroy,
And strike to Dust th'aspiring Tow'rs of *Troy*;
Steel cou'd the works of mortal Pride confound,
140 And hew Triumphal Arches to the ground.
What Wonder then, fair Nymph! thy Hairs shou'd feel
The conqu'ring Force of unresisted Steel?

Canto II

But anxious Cares the pensive Nymph opprest,
And secret Passions labour'd in her Breast.
Not youthful Kings in Battle seiz'd alive,
Not scornful Virgins who their Charms survive,
Not ardent Lover robb'd of all his Bliss,
Not ancient Lady when refus'd a Kiss,
Not Tyrants fierce that unrepenting die,
Not *Cynthia* when her *Manteau's* pinn'd awry,
E'er felt such Rage, Resentment, and Despair,
10 As Thou, sad Virgin! for thy ravish'd Hair.

While her rackt Soul Repose and Peace requires,
The fierce *Thalestris* fans the rising Fires.
O wretched Maid (she spread her hands, and cry'd,
And *Hampton's* Ecchoes, wretched Maid! reply'd)
Was it for this you took such constant Care,
Combs, Bodkins, Leads, Pomatums, to prepare?
For this your Locks in Paper Durance bound,
For this with tort'ring Irons wreath'd around?
Oh had the Youth but been content to seize
20 Hairs less in sight—or any Hairs but these!
Gods! shall the Ravisher display this Hair,
While the Fops envy, and the Ladies stare!
Honour forbid! at whose unrival'd Shrine
Ease, Pleasure, Virtue, All, our Sex resign.

Methinks already I your Tears survey,
Already hear the horrid things they say,
Already see you a degraded Toast,
And all your Honour in a Whisper lost!
How shall I, then, your helpless Fame defend?
30 'Twill then be Infamy to seem your Friend!
And shall this Prize, th' inestimable Prize,
Expos'd thro' *Crystal* to the gazing Eyes,
And heightened by the *Diamond's* circling Rays,
On that Rapacious Hand for ever blaze?
Sooner shall grass in *Hide-Park Circus* grow,
And Wits take Lodgings in the Sound of *Bow*;
Sooner let Earth, Air, Sea, to *Chaos* fall,
Men, Monkies, Lap-dogs, Parrots, perish all!

She said; then raging to *Sir Plume* repairs,
40 And bids her *Beau* demand the precious Hairs:
(*Sir Plume*, of *Amber Snuff-box* justly vain,
And the nice Conduct of a *clouded Cane*)
With earnest Eyes, and round unthinking Face,
He first the Snuff-box open'd, then the Case,
And thus broke out – 'My Lord, why, what the Devil?
'Z——ds! damn the Lock! 'fore Gad, you must be civil
'Plague on't! 'tis past a Jest – nay prithee, Pox!
'Give her the Hair' – he spoke, and rapp'd his Box.

It grieves me much (reply'd the Peer again)
50 Who speaks so well shou'd ever speak in vain.
But by this Locke, this sacred Locke I swear,
(Which never more shall join its parted Hair,
Which never more its Honours shall renew,
Clip'd from the lovely Head where once it grew)
That while my Nostrils draw the vital Air,
This Hand, which won it, shall for ever wear.
He spoke, and speaking, in proud Triumph spread
The long-contended Honours of her Head.

But see! the *Nymph* in Sorrow's Pomp appears,
60 Her Eyes half-languishing, half-drown'd in Tears;
Now livid pale her Cheeks, now glowing red;

On her heav'd Bosom hung her drooping Head,
Which, with a Sigh, she rais'd; and thus she said.

For ever curs'd be this detested Day,
Which snatch'd my best, my fav'rite Curl away!
Happy! ah ten times happy, had I been,
If *Hampton-Court* these Eyes had never seen!
Yet am not I the first mistaken Maid,
By Love of Courts to num'rous Ills betray'd.
70 Oh had I rather un-admir'd remain'd
In some lone *Isle*, or distant *Northern* Land;
Where the gilt *Chariot* never mark'd the way,
Where none learn *Ombre*, none e'er taste *Bohea*!
There kept my Charms conceal'd from mortal Eye,
Like Roses, that in Desarts bloom and die.
What mov'd my Mind with youthful Lords to rome?
O had I stay'd, and said my Pray'rs at home!
'Twas this, the Morning *Omens* did foretel;
Thrice from my trembling hand the *Patch-box* fell;
80 The tott'ring *China* shook without a Wind,
Nay, *Poll* sat, mute, and *Shock* was *most Unkind*!
See the poor Remnants of this slighted Hair!
My hands shall rend what ev'n thy own did spare.
This, in two sable Ringlets taught to break,
Once gave new Beauties to the snowie Neck;
The Sister-Locke now sits uncouth, alone,
And in its Fellow's Fate foresees its own;
Uncurl'd it hangs! the fatal Sheers demands;
And tempts once more thy sacrilegious Hands.

90 She said: the pitying Audience melt in Tears,
But *Fate* and *Jove* had stopp'd the *Baron's* ears.
In vain *Thalestris* with Reproach assails,
For who can move when fair *Belinda* fails?
Not half so fix'd the *Trojan* cou'd remain,
While *Anna* begg'd and *Dido* rag'd in vain.
To Arms, to Arms! the bold *Thalestris* cries,
And swift as Lightning to the Combate flies.
All side in Parties, and begin th'Attack;
Fans clap, Silks russle and tough whalebones crack;

100   Heroes and Heroins Shouts confus'dly rise,
       And base, and treble Voices strike the Skies.
       No common Weapons in their Hands are found,
       Like Gods they fight, nor dread a mortal Wound.

       So when bold *Homer* makes the Gods engage,
       And heav'nly Breasts with human Passions rage;
       'Gainst *Pallas, Mars;. Latona, Hermes* Arms;
       And all *Olympus* rings with loud Alarms.
       Jove's Thunder roars, Heav'n trembles all around;
       Blue *Neptune* storms, the bellowing Deeps resound;
110   *Earth* shakes her nodding Tow'rs, the Ground gives way,
       And the pale Ghosts start at the Flash of Day!

       While thro' the Press enrag'd *Thalestris* flies,
       And scatters Deaths around from both her Eyes,
       A *Beau* and *Witling* perish'd in the Throng,
       One dy'd in *Metaphor*, and one in *Song*.
       O cruel Nymph! a living Death I bear
       Cry'd *Dapperwit*, and sunk beside his Chair.
       A mournful Glance *Sir Fopling* upwards cast,
       Those eyes are made so killing – was his last:
120   Thus on *Meander's* flow'ry Margin lies
       Th' expiring Swan, and as he sings he dies.

       As bold Sir *Plume* had drawn *Clarissa* down,
       Chloë stept in, and kill'd him with a Frown;
       She smil'd to see the doughty Hero slain,
       But at her Smile, the Beau reviv'd again.

       Now *Jove* suspends his golden Scales in Air,
       Weighs the Mens Wits against the Lady's Hair;
       The doubtful Beam long nods from side to side;
       At length the Wits mount up, the Hairs subside.

130   See Fierce *Belinda* on the *Baron* flies,
       With more than usual Lightning in her Eyes;
       Nor fear'd the Chief th'unequal Fight to try,
       Who sought no more than on his Foe to die.
       But this bold Lord, with manly Strength indu'd,

She with one Finger and a Thumb subdu'd:
Just where the breath of Life his Nostrils drew,
A Charge of *Snuff* the wily Virgin threw;
Sudden, with starting Tears each Eye o'erflows,
And the high Dome re-ecchoes to his Nose.

140 Now meet thy Fate, th'incens'd Virago cry'd,
And drew a deadly *Bodkin* from her Side.
Boast not my Fall (he said) insulting Foe!
Thou by some other shalt be laid as low.
Nor think, to dye dejects my lofty Mind:
All that I dread, is leaving you behind!
Rather than so, ah let me still survive,
And still burn on, in *Cupid's* Flames, *Alive.*

 Restore the Locke! she cries; and all around
Restore the Locke! the vaulted Roofs rebound.
150 Not fierce *Othello* in so loud a Strain
Roar'd for the Handkerchief that caus'd his Pain.
But see! how oft Ambitious Aims are cross'd,
And Chiefs contend 'till all the Prize is lost!
The Locke, obtain'd with Guilt, and kept with Pain,
In ev'ry place is sought, but sought in vain:
With such a Prize no Mortal must be blest,
So Heav'n decrees! with Heav'n who can contest?

 Some thought, it mounted to the Lunar Sphere,
Since all that Man e'er lost, is treasur'd there.
160 There Heroe's Wits are kept in pondrous Vases,
And Beau's in *Snuff-boxes* and *Tweezer-Cases.*
There broken Vows, and Death-bed Alms are found,
And Lovers Hearts with Ends of Riband bound;
The Courtiers Promises, and Sick Man's Pray'rs,
The Smiles of Harlots, and the Tears of Heirs,
Cages for Gnats, and Chains to Yoak a Flea;
Dry'd Butterflies, and Tomes of Casuistry.

 But trust the Muse—she saw it upward rise,
Tho' mark'd by none but quick Poetic Eyes:
170 (Thus *Rome's* great Founder to the Heav'ns withdrew,

To *Proculus* alone confess'd in view.)
A sudden Star, it shot thro' liquid Air,
And drew behind a radiant *Trail of Hair.*
Not *Berenice's* Locks first rose so bright,
The Skies bespangling with dishevel'd Light.
This, the *Beau-monde* shall from the *Mall* survey,
As thro' the Moon-light shade they nightly stray,
And hail with Musick its propitious Ray.
This *Partridge* soon shall view in cloudless Skies,
180   When next he looks thro' *Galilæo's* Eyes;
And hence th'Egregious Wizard shall foredoom
The Fate of *Louis*, and the Fall of *Rome.*

   Then cease, bright Nymph! to mourn the ravish'd Hair,
Which adds new Glory to the shining Sphere!
Not all the Tresses that fair Head can boast,
Shall draw such Envy as the Locke you lost.
For, after all the Murders of your Eye,
When, after Millions slain, your self shall die;
When those fair Suns shall sett, as sett they must,
190   And all those Tresses shall be laid in Dust;
This Locke, the Muse shall consecrate to Fame,
And mid'st the Stars inscribe *Belinda's* Name!

FINIS

Appendix 3

Pope's first translation of Sarpedon's battle speech was published as early as 1709. He made only minor changes when, years later, he incorporated the passage into his translation of the *Iliad*. It is this speech which Clarissa's advice in Canto V mocks and emulates.

Sarpedon to Glaucus

     Why boast we, *Glaucus*, our extended Reign
Where *Xanthus*' Streams enrich the *Lycian* Plain?
Our num'rous Herds that range each fruitful Field,
And Hills where Vines their Purple Harvest yield?
Our foaming Bowls with gen'rous *Nectar* crown'd,
Our Feasts enhanc'd with Musick's sprightly Sound?
Why on these Shores are we with Joy survey'd,
Admir'd as Heroes, and as Gods obey'd?
Unless great Acts superior Merit prove,
10 And Vindicate the bounteous Powr's above:
'Tis ours, the Dignity They give, to grace;
The first in Valour, as the first in Place:
That while with wondring Eyes our Martial Bands
Behold our Deeds transcending our Commands,
Such, they may cry, deserve the Sov'reign State,
Whom those that Envy dare not Imitate!
Cou'd all our Care elude the greedy Grave,
Which claims no less the Fearful than the Brave,
For Lust of Fame I shou'd not vainly dare
20 In fighting Fields, nor urge thy Soul to War.
But since, alas, ignoble Age must come,
Disease, and Death's inexorable doom;
The Life which others pay, let Us bestow,
And give to Fame what we to Nature owe;
Brave, tho' we fall; and honour'd, if we live;
Or let us Glory gain, or Glory give!